# A MIGHTY LONG WAY

# A MIGHTY LONG WAY

## MY JOURNEY TO JUSTICE
## AT LITTLE ROCK CENTRAL HIGH SCHOOL

### ADAPTED FOR YOUNG READERS

## Carlotta Walls LaNier

with **Lisa Frazier Page**

A YEARLING BOOK

Text copyright © 2023 by Carlotta Walls LaNier
Cover photograph copyright © Will Counts Collection, Indiana University Archives

This work is based on *A Mighty Long Way: My Journey to Justice at Little Rock Central High School*,
copyright © 2009 by Carlotta Walls LaNier. Published in hardcover in the United States by One
World, an imprint of Random House, a division of Penguin Random House LLC, New York, in 2009.

Yearling and the jumping horse design are
registered trademarks of Penguin Random House LLC.

Title page photograph: Will Counts Collection, Indiana University Archives

Visit us on the Web! rhcbooks.com

Educators and librarians, for a variety of teaching tools, visit us at RHTeachersLibrarians.com

LCCN 2023285256
ISBN 978-0-593-48675-7 (hardcover) — ISBN 978-0-593-48676-4 (lib. bdg.) —
ISBN 978-0-593-48677-1 (ebook) — ISBN 978-0-593-48678-8 (paperback)

Editor: Beverly Horowitz
Editorial Assistant: Rebecca Gudelis
Cover Designer: Ray Shappell
Interior Designer: Ken Crossland
Paperback Designer: Jinna Shin
Copy Editor: Colleen Fellingham
Managing Editor: Tamar Schwartz
Production Manager: Natalia Dextre

Printed in the United States of America
1st Printing
First Yearling Edition 2024

Random House Children's Books supports the First Amendment
and celebrates the right to read.

This book is dedicated to my parents, Juanita and Cartelyou Walls, who taught me determination, commitment, and perseverance so I could take the journey with confidence.

To my sisters, Loujuana and Tina, who learned the same lessons and took them to another level. My love for you is immeasurable. You share in every bit of recognition I receive.

To my comrades, who shared the journey with strength and courage:

Ernest Green

Minnijean Brown

Elizabeth Eckford

Thelma Mothershed

Melba Pattillo

Gloria Ray

Terrence Roberts

the late Jefferson Thomas

To my loving husband, Ira (Ike), whose support, patience, and wisdom have encouraged me to stay on track.

To my son and daughter, Whitney and Brooke, who continue to bring me joy. I am glad I completed the journey so that you could explore your own paths freely and with conviction. Carry on, knowing that you have my unconditional love.

And to generations yet unborn who will adopt the spirit and carry on the Walls-Cullins-LaNier legacies.

# INTRODUCTION

For three years, I turned down invitations from a history teacher to speak to her class at a high school about thirty miles from my home in Denver, Colorado. I had put my painful past as one of nine students who integrated Little Rock Central High School in Arkansas in 1957 far behind me. And I didn't want to talk about it.

One day, though, the teacher said something that changed my mind.

"They need to hear from you," she said.

It was 1987, and thirty years had passed since the days when my eight black classmates and I became known to the world as the Little Rock Nine. The country had changed. People were reflecting on the lessons learned during a time of such racial division that the President of the United States had to send the military to protect the nine of us black students from crowds of angry white citizens who did not want their children to attend school with us.

I visited a school and shared my story publicly for the first time with the students. You will learn the details of that story in this book. When I finished, a student in the back of the classroom raised his hand. His face was red with anger and embarrassment—a look I will never forget—as he asked: "Why am I just learning this? Why haven't I learned this in school before now?"

The student's question helped me to realize that, despite my pain, I needed to do more to let the next generations of students know what happened in Little Rock and how great sacrifices made by nine courageous young people, our families, and allies helped to ensure that *all* students, regardless of their race, have access to the best education possible. This book helps to further that mission. And as a grandmother to two young readers, I am excited to share this part of my journey with you.

# PROLOGUE

### Remembering Central High—
### More Than Sixty Years Later

All that week, I managed to stay calm.

Through the touching speeches by politicians and civil rights leaders. Through the fancy meals at the Arkansas Governor's Mansion. Through a play that told the story of the Little Rock Nine. Even when I saw the new visitors' center for the high school, where the real-life drama had taken place fifty years ago.

Screens played black-and-white television footage from that day—September 25, 1957. But something wouldn't let me linger. I didn't want to see the fourteen-year-old black girl climbing those steps in her new, store-bought outfit. I didn't want to see her surrounded by armed military men who had been ordered by the president to guard her from the spitting, clawing white mob. I didn't want to know her fear again.

Then, on the last day of the events celebrating the

fiftieth anniversary of the Little Rock Nine, President Bill Clinton cracked my armor. As I sat near the very steps that I had climbed five decades earlier, the former president's words took me back. He was talking about courage, gratitude, and the responsibility that each of us has to contribute to the world, to do something more than talk, even when stepping up comes at a cost. He turned slightly away from the podium and looked sideways at us, the men and women seated behind him.

"These nine people didn't just have an opinion," he said. "They didn't just say, 'Wouldn't it be nice if someone did something to change things.' These nine people and their families stepped up and said, 'Here am I, Lord, send me.'"

My lips started to quiver. Instinctively, my hands went up to cover them, as though they were a shield, as though they could keep back all the memories and pain. I thought about Mother sitting out there in the audience, still beautiful and elegant at eighty-two. And I remembered watching her soft, jet-black hair turn gray during that tumultuous and uncertain school year.

I thought about Daddy, a devoted family man and World War II veteran who didn't live long enough to see this day. And I remembered the chilling fear that crept into my soul late one night when the FBI took him away for questioning after our home was mysteriously bombed during my senior year. I thought, too, about Herbert, my childhood friend and neighbor, who was convicted by an all-white jury for the bombing and served nearly two years in a maximum-security prison for a crime that I believe wholeheartedly he did not commit. I looked to my left and right on the stage and caught glimpses of my eight comrades, my dear friends, some of whom are now grandparents. We'd come a mighty long way, and all nine of us were still here. By now, nothing could keep back the tears.

*Here am I, Lord, send me.*

The U.S. Supreme Court had ordered American schools to desegregate in its 1954 *Brown v. Board of Education* decision. Southern states raged against this decree, and the state of Arkansas was no exception. But as much as the local school system dug in its heels, integration was the law of the land.

I hadn't intended anything heroic when I signed up to attend Little Rock Central High School. I didn't even know much about it besides that it was close to my home and, at the time, all white. In the spring of 1957, my ninth-grade teacher at the all-black Dunbar Junior High School passed around a sheet of paper to sign if we were interested in attending Central the next fall. I did so without hesitation. I didn't ask my parents' permission or even mention it to them right away. It was just a given that

I would pursue the top-quality education that Mother and Daddy had always preached about at home. But that simple declaration changed the course of my life, of my family's, and of countless black students' for generations to come.

The change would have to be forced, though. Staunch segregationists throughout Little Rock—including Arkansas governor Orval Faubus—refused with all their might to accept integration. President Dwight D. Eisenhower ultimately sent the U.S. military to escort the nine of us to integrate Central High School for the first time. White students ostracized and harassed us daily, and many teachers looked the other way.

Soon enough we came to be known around the world as the Little Rock Nine.

Eight of us survived that turbulent first year. But for me, the story did not end there. After the governor shut down all three of Little Rock's high schools to avoid integration, only two of the original nine of us returned to Central. I was one of them, and that was my senior year. Then, just three months before my graduation, my home was bombed. My father and a childhood friend were targeted as suspects by an unjust legal system. But I persevered through it all and became the first black girl ever to walk across the stage to receive a diploma from Little Rock Central High School.

The morning after my graduation, I took the first train out of Little Rock and promised never to look back. Shaken by the traumatic bombing and its aftermath, the rest of my family soon followed. We eventually settled in Denver, Colorado, which felt about as far away from home as we could get, in both distance and character. There, I met my husband, Ira, and raised two children: a son, Whitney, and a daughter, Brooke.

For thirty years, I didn't utter a public word about what had happened to me and my comrades at the place once known as "America's Most Beautiful School." I rarely even talked about it at home. To this day, Mother and I still have never sat down and held a serious conversation about that time. Part of it, I suspect, is that we're not prone to dwell in the past, examine our feelings publicly, or show much emotion. The wounds opened in Little Rock—I've come to realize—are deep and, in some cases, still raw.

I've pushed myself to remember, even when I didn't want to. It's a commitment I made to myself in 1987, the first time the nine of us returned all together to Little Rock Central High School. The National Association for the Advancement of Colored People (NAACP)—a stalwart civil rights organization—was holding its annual meeting in Little Rock to commemorate the thirtieth anniversary of the city's school desegregation battle. It was the first time I had seen most of my comrades since we'd left Central, and my first trip back to the school since my graduation. As I walked through those halls, it was almost as if I could hear those vile words bouncing off the walls again: *nigger . . . nigger . . . nigger.* Again, I could see the contorted faces of my classmates and their snickers and jeers. I could feel the slimy wet spit. For a moment, it felt as though it might suffocate me. I realized then that even though I had built a new life almost a thousand miles away, I hadn't moved an inch from Little Rock.

Late that night, after the NAACP event, Governor—and soon to be president—Bill Clinton invited the nine of us to join him at his home in the Governor's Mansion. His wife, Hillary, greeted us warmly and escorted us to her kitchen table. We sat there for hours, until about three a.m., chatting like old friends. Governor Clinton told us that as a sixth grader growing up not far away in Hope, Arkansas, in 1957, he had rooted for us. He said that we inspired him and significantly impacted how he viewed race. I was touched by the couple's genuine curiosity and interest. That conversation helped me to open up and talk freely about my experience for the first time. The reunion also reconnected the nine of us, some of whom had been strangers to one another when our fates first intertwined at Central. We pledged to stay in touch—a promise that has yielded deep and enduring friendships. The experience also set me on a quest for healing and a greater understanding of what we had been through.

This book is the result of that journey.

It is as much a story about family, perseverance, and sacrifice as it is about history. It is a salute to my parents, Cartelyou and Juanita Walls, who ingrained in me the quiet confidence that, Jim Crow be damned, I was not a second-class citizen. It was that confidence that told me: I deserve the high-quality education the Supreme Court said I was due. And it was that confidence that steadied my feet to defy the racists at school every single day. My parents bequeathed to me the confidence of their fathers, both hardworking black entrepreneurs. My family may have seemed unlikely candidates for sparking change across the nation. But then again, that is the point of this book: to show that determination, fortitude, and the ability to move the world aren't reserved for the "special" people.

My comrades and I started a nonprofit foundation called the Little Rock Nine Foundation. We created a scholarship program to help send young people of color to college. Each of us has taken on the responsibility of mentoring the first group of scholarship winners. The plan is for our first group of scholars to mentor our next group, and so on. In this way, we will touch the lives of children for generations to come and leave behind a legacy that extends far beyond Little Rock Central High School.

In the public mind, Ernest, Melba, Minnijean, Elizabeth, Gloria, Terrence, the late Jefferson, Thelma, and I are one, the Little Rock Nine. But we are, in essence, nine distinct personalities with nine different stories.

This book shares mine.

# CHAPTER 1

## A Different World

For the longest time, I wanted nothing more to do with Little Rock. After leaving in 1960, I returned only when necessary. But my work as president of the Little Rock Nine Foundation would bring me home often. Inevitably, I would wind down Interstate 630 to my old neighborhood. Most often, I would go there to see Uncle Teet, who lived in my great-great-grandfather Hiram Holloway's old house, five houses down from the one where I grew up. But every now and then, I would pull up alongside the redbrick bungalow at Fifteenth and Valentine Streets, park the car, and get out.

This was the center of my world as a child. The place looks abandoned with its boarded-up windows and weeds, where lush green grass used to grow. There is no sign of the big gardenia bush that once stood in the front yard. Mother would pick a fresh flower from that bush and place it in her hair just so, like the singer Billie Holiday. But the gardenias are long gone. So, too, is the tree in the backyard that used to grow the plumpest, sweetest figs around. The pecan tree still stands, and as I picked up a few dried nuts one scorching summer day, I was reminded of the Christmas in junior high school when that tree provided perfect homemade gifts for most of my family and friends. Money was tight that year, so I made date nut cakes from the bounty in our backyard to give away as presents.

I'm amazed at how small it all seems now—our house, the yard, and even those pecan trees, which to a little girl staring up seemed just a few steps from heaven. I still call the place "our house," as if it remains in my family. But Mother finally sold it many years ago when the upkeep became too much and I convinced her that none of her three girls would ever return. She was reluctant at first to let go. The memories, I guess. And our family roots—they run pretty deep through there.

I was three years old when Daddy bought the house at 1500 South Valentine Street, just blocks away from the all-white Central High School. Even then, the school was known throughout the country for its Greek-inspired architecture, beauty, and high academic achievement. Daddy had just returned from the Philippines, where he served in World War II until December 1945. My parents paid $3,000 for the house, sold to them by my mother's grandfather, Aaron Holloway, who had raised her practically all her life.

Papa Holloway, as I knew my great-grandfather, had tan skin, dark eyes, thick, wavy black hair, and a mustache. I'm told that in his younger days, his hair would sprout into a nest of thick black curls. Our neighbors called him Curly. He stood about six feet tall, and family members say that I—tall and skinny as a child—inherited his height and build. I probably inherited some of his other characteristics, too, like my hair, which, when I was a child, was so long and thick that I had trouble grooming it. Mother had to plait it into neat braids or pull it into ponytails until I was well into junior high school. I wasn't allowed to get my first haircut until eighth grade, and I've mostly kept it short ever since.

The Spanish roots in my family tree can be traced back to Papa Holloway's father, Hiram. I never knew him, but in recent years I've read interviews he did in the 1930s for a collection of ex-slave narratives. Hiram was described in the report as a "tri-racial free person of color," born in 1848, about thirteen years before the Civil War. He said in a transcript of the interview that his mother was a "full-blooded Cherokee" and his father a "dark Spaniard." He used the N-word liberally as he talked about the Africans who were enslaved. That word still stings when I see or hear it, but I've tried to refrain from harsh judgment of my great-great-grandfather, even as he set himself apart from the enslaved Africans. As difficult as some parts of his story were to digest, the interview reminded me just how much my ancestors endured in their pursuit of education, generations before I ever stepped foot into Central.

"In slave times, they didn't have any schools for niggers," said Hiram, who nevertheless managed to learn to read and write. "Niggers better not be caught with a book. If he were caught with a book, they beat him to death nearly . . . They didn't allow no free niggers to go to school either in slave times."

Hiram's story gave me fresh insight into how much my family valued education even then. I wanted to know more about them. Once, I asked Papa Holloway about his brothers and sisters. He told me he had several siblings but that he was in touch with only one, a sister, Maude, who lived in Cleveland. He said that he suspected his other brothers and sisters were scattered throughout the country and passed as white. But Papa Holloway identified himself as "colored" and was proud of the status he achieved as one of the first "colored" building contractors in Arkansas. He helped to build houses throughout the state, and even built White Memorial Methodist Church, where my family worshipped. Most Sundays, I sat proudly beside Papa on the front pew.

Papa's wife, Mary, died in 1922 at age thirty-four while

giving birth to their sixteenth child. The baby girl died, too, as did a set of twins who had been born earlier. Papa raised the remaining children and never married again. His oldest son, Hugh, would become one of only two black men who worked as skilled laborers on Central High School when it was built. Papa's longtime girlfriend, Dora Holmes, was a widow who lived down the street and owned the house at 1500 South Valentine Street. When Mrs. Holmes died, she left her estate in the care of Papa Holloway, who offered the house to my father.

None of us could have imagined then how much that house would dictate the course of our lives in the years ahead. The house was just west of downtown Little Rock, not too far from Ninth Street, a bustling strip of black-owned businesses and nightspots. The community surrounding Ninth Street was all black. My end of town was more racially mixed—black families lived on one block, whites on the other. In some cases, black and white families lived across the street from one another. But our white neighbors may as well have been living on Mars for all we knew of their lives. Most of the houses in the neighborhood were box-shaped with wooden frames, modest but well kept. A few had porches, and most had small yards, though they didn't seem small then. Our house stood out because Daddy, who earned a living as a brick mason, meticulously covered it from top to bottom with the same red bricks that remain on the house today. The only other brick house in the neighborhood belonged to Papa Holloway.

Daddy had learned the brick masonry trade from his father-in-law, Med Cullins, a master contractor who did brick masonry work on Central High in the 1940s. Grandpa Cullins, my mother's father, was a real character. He was a big, imposing man who stood over six feet tall with a heavyset frame, a gravelly voice, and a gruff disposition that matched his size. His beige skin and straight hair gave him the appearance of a slightly tanned white man. He walked with his shoulders squared and head high. Grandpa was his own man. He had one suit and wore mismatched socks, but he considered those kinds of things trivial. Confidence seemed to radiate from him.

Grandpa was not a patient man. He called every man "son" and every woman "daughter," including his own children and grandchildren, who say he did so because he didn't want to bother remembering any names.

"Daughter, let me speak to daughter," he commanded one day when I answered the phone at home.

I looked at Mother and my aunt, who was visiting us that day, and responded: "Which one?"

"Goddammit," Grandpa barked. "The one who lives there!"

Grandpa Cullins was an intellectual man who had

insisted that his four children—Mother, her younger brother, and two older sisters—go to college. Grandpa loved politics, particularly presidential history. Many times, I heard him start with Truman and work his way back, reciting the years each president served, the president's party, and something significant about each man's time in office.

All my grandfathers outlived their wives. While I was nurtured by a cadre of well-educated and loving women, I spent a lot of time around the men on both sides of my family. And they heavily influenced the woman I became. The independent streak that I'm sure I inherited from my grandfathers would land me at Central soon enough, and the determination I witnessed in them would help me survive the toughest days at school and onward.

No one was more determined than my Big Daddy. He was Porter Walls, my father's father. He had mahogany skin and a medium build and was on the shorter side. He had only a third-grade education, but he could read and write and was one of the smartest businessmen I've ever known. He owned and operated a pool hall and restaurant a short walk from my house. Big Daddy enjoyed looking like a businessman, so his preferred attire was a suit and hat when he wasn't in the kitchen. He also smoked cigars.

Daddy had helped his father build the business and

worked there part-time. Big Daddy worked at Arkansas Tent and Awnings during the day, while his sisters ran the café. But he split his nights and weekends between the café and pool hall and poured all his energy and every extra dime into building his business.

It wasn't until I was grown that I truly understood the source of his drive and persistence. It was 1977, and *Roots,* the television miniseries based on Alex Haley's novel, had a grip on America. People everywhere sat glued to their televisions night after night, and many black men and women for the first time began digging into their own family trees. I was deeply moved by the drama, which chronicled the life of a young West African man captured from his native land and sold into slavery in the southern United States. All of a sudden, I also was filled with questions about my southern family, and the violent enslavement they had endured.

My questions started with my grandpa, Big Daddy. "Tell me the story of the Walls family," I said to him one day when I caught him alone.

Big Daddy looked up at me, surprisingly annoyed. "Why do you want to know all that?" he snapped.

Big Daddy was usually a warm, patient man, and he and I were close, having spent much time together throughout my childhood. But he knew what I was getting at, and he was no fan of all the modern talk about slavery and our people needing to discover their African roots. Just a couple of generations removed from the hateful violence and degradation of slavery, he was not eager to remember. The past was the past, Big Daddy figured. No need to dig up long-buried bones. He paused, and finally, peering straight into my eyes, he said:

"Look, all you really need to know is my grandfather owned land."

The seriousness in Big Daddy's eyes told me he had nothing more to say. What, if anything, he knew of slavery in his family, he wasn't willing to share. But he was lucky that somehow in the shadow of the nation's most brutal system of oppression, his family had managed to accumulate valuable land. That knowledge, that pride, would push him toward his own dreams of owning a business. Eventually, Big Daddy opened a second restaurant and pool hall on the outskirts of Little Rock, retired from his day job, and became his own boss.

Historical records show that Big Daddy's great-grandfather Richard was born during slavery. It is unclear how Richard's son Coatney came to own more than 360 wooded acres in Cornerville, the town where the Walls family first settled, about seventy-five miles south of Little Rock. But when Coatney Walls died, the land was divided and passed on in equal shares to his heirs—Big Daddy and each of his seven younger siblings.

In many ways, Big Daddy was ahead of his time. He seemed to have an innate understanding of money and power. All he ever wanted to be was a businessman, a powerful man. He had volunteered for World War I in 1918. When he returned home to Henrietta, the girlfriend he'd left behind, he saw a toddler playing outside. The child was his son. This wasn't the life he had planned, but he did the proper thing and married Henrietta. The couple eventually moved to Little Rock and had four more boys and two girls. Their third-born was Cartelyou, my father.

Big Daddy worked hard and put aside whatever money he could. At home, he ruled with an iron fist and pushed his children to work hard, too, particularly the older boys. The older two sons could hardly wait until they were grown enough to take the train out of Little Rock and move on to lives of their own making. But Cartelyou stayed, working at his father's side, soaking in his father's work ethic and values.

Cartelyou was fifteen when his mother, Henrietta, just thirty-nine years old, died of pneumonia. He grieved mightily and clung to his sisters for support. Soon enough, his younger sister, Margaret, introduced him to one of her friends, a petite, fair-skinned beauty named Juanita. Juanita Cullins was a fellow student at Paul Laurence Dunbar Junior and Senior High School, the premier black high school in Arkansas. It was love at first sight, and on February 3, 1942, the teenagers eloped with another couple to Benton, Arkansas. They were married by a justice of the peace.

Cartelyou was shipped off to World War II on December 7 that year. Eleven days later, I was born. To support us, Mother got a job downtown at M. M. Cohn Department Store, where she worked as a seamstress and clerk, mostly altering customers' newly purchased clothes. As a black woman, she was not permitted to touch the cash register or receive credit for a sale. Likewise, black customers could shop in the store but were not permitted to try on clothes or return them. Mother, as soft-spoken and dignified as she was good-looking, never complained out loud.

When Daddy returned from the war, she mostly stayed home. She also continued her education at the renowned historically black college Philander Smith, though she stopped short of graduating. Whenever money was tight, she helped out by getting a job, usually as a secretary.

Big Daddy often babysat me, and I loved spending time with him. He was quiet but attentive, much like my father. I always wanted to be near him. My favorite place to hang out was the restaurant, where I could have all the cold drinks and candy I wanted. But the pool hall was off-limits to me. When I got sleepy, I stepped outside, climbed into the back seat of Big Daddy's car, and stretched out, feeling safe and protected. Every time I opened my eyes, it seemed, I could see through the car window the silhouette of Big Daddy, a cigar clenched between his teeth and a pool stick in hand, standing in the darkness, checking on his grandbaby.

As I grew older, Big Daddy let me tag along when he went to the meatpacking houses downtown. He went to buy boxes of ribs and fish for the barbecue dinners and fried catfish plates that had made his restaurant and pool hall so popular. As soon as Big Daddy opened the door to the meatpacking house, I could smell the thick scent of raw meat. A round white man wearing a sleeveless shirt and dingy white apron stood behind the counter. His bare arms looked beefy and pale. I sauntered behind Big Daddy as he walked straight up to the counter. My grandfather seemed to stand taller there, as white customers came in and out. I watched quietly as Big Daddy exchanged a few amicable words with the white man, who spoke without a hiss or word of disrespect. When it came time to pay, Big Daddy dug into his pocket and pulled out a huge wad of cash. Big Daddy passed a few bills into the hands of the white man, nodded a silent thank-you, and turned to walk away. I trailed behind him proudly, thinking to myself that Big Daddy must be a rich, important man to get such respect from white folks.

Big Daddy's personality and style were as different from those of Grandpa Cullins as was his appearance. But both men deeply respected each other, so much so that each addressed the other as "Mr. Walls" or "Mr. Cullins." They shared a love of baseball—and, more specifically, the Brooklyn Dodgers, Jackie Robinson's team. In 1947, the Dodgers had become the first team to integrate professional baseball. Jackie was my two grandpas' hero, and he became mine, too.

Whenever the Dodgers played in St. Louis, the family piled into the car for a road trip to the game. We most often left late at night and traveled until morning without stopping. That was because hotels and restaurants throughout the South refused to admit black folks. Daddy would map out the eight-hour trip so that we could stop at relatives' homes for bathroom breaks and rest along the way.

Back home in Little Rock, my entire family looked forward to watching baseball teams from the Negro Leagues play in Fair Park. It seemed like every person of color from the West End was headed to the game. I was in elementary school then, and those trips to the park were like going to the circus. It never occurred to me as I grew up to question why colored folks could go to the park only on certain days, why we had to climb to the back of the bus, or why even stopping at a gas station to use the bathroom in most areas of the South wasn't an option. Those were the rules. I learned to follow them like I learned to walk: by observing those closest to me and following their lead until I knew the steps well enough to venture out on my own. The world I knew best—a black world full of protective family, neighbors, and my church community—felt safe. There, I knew I was loved and accepted.

On the playground, a few of my darker-skinned playmates took to calling me "high yella" because of my light complexion. They wondered if I thought that my skin's white tint made me better than them. They themselves had been affected by colorism, and the many ways darker-skinned folks are treated significantly worse than lighter-skinned folks, tracing all the way back to the era of slavery. In my mind, that cruel, racist phenomenon should have never been the case to begin with. And the skin-color separation just seemed silly. My family members were every hue, from pinkish white to rich brown.

At that age, Daddy and Big Daddy were my protectors. Mother was, too. When racism and bigotry surfaced around us, my parents and grandfather tried to explain. They wanted to make sure I understood that I was not the problem.

I must have been in elementary school the first time I felt the sting of a white woman's words. Mother and I were on a crowded bus when a white woman stepped on. She quickly scanned the bus and rolled her eyes.

"These nigras are all over the place," she blurted as she took a seat.

The anger on her face and the huffiness in her voice

told me her words were not nice. Somehow, I knew they were directed at me, at those of us sitting in the back. I looked up at Mother, with a face that all my life has shown exactly what I'm thinking. In that moment, my eyes probably asked: What does she mean? What did *we* do wrong?

At first, Mother said nothing, as if she didn't even hear it. Then, ever so discreetly, she pulled me closer to her and whispered: "Carlotta, we must be patient with ignorance and never, ever bring ourselves down to their level."

I would hear those words many times, too, from Daddy, like when he didn't respond to a white man who uttered something disrespectful: *You are a Walls. You must never, ever stoop to the level of ignorance.*

I came to believe that *they*—mean and intolerant people—were the ones with the problem and that I must never, ever *stoop* to their level. That lesson would shield me in the years ahead when I came face-to-face with the ugliest side of that cruel world.

Until then, I played by rules I knew. I'd never seen the game played any other way.

Then came New York.

I could hardly believe my ears when my parents told me near the end of third grade in 1951 that I'd be going to that great city for the summer. Daddy's younger sister, Juanita, and her husband Alfredo had invited me to spend my three-month break from school with them. I felt as if a fairy godmother had waved a magic wand

and granted me a dream summer vacation. I had heard Mother brag about New York practically all my life. Her eyes seemed to light up when she talked to her friends about the time she'd visited New York with her sister in 1944, going out late and staying in an apartment building in Sugar Hill, the ritzy section of Harlem. From the 1920s, when wealthy black men and women began migrating there, through the 1960s, Sugar Hill was home to some of the nation's best-known black scholars, writers, activists, sports figures, and entertainers: W. E. B. Du Bois, Langston Hughes, Zora Neale Hurston, Duke Ellington, Joe Louis, Thurgood Marshall. Aunt Juanita's first apartment in New York was there, too.

The anticipation of seeing the high-rises and bright lights of the city and of Sugar Hill left me so excited about my trip that I couldn't even bother being scared.

My parents summoned their friends to keep watch over me during the trip. Like Herman Freeman—Uncle Herman to me—who worked as a redcap at the Little Rock station. My parents also were good friends with the head cook on the train, Aubrey Yancy. My classmate's father, Mr. Murchison, a porter on the route to St. Louis, had agreed to be my guardian for most of the trip. As protective as my parents were, they trusted that I was in good hands. The connections among black rail workers throughout the country back then operated like a modern-day Underground Railroad, assuring the safe transport and comfort of one another's family and friends.

The day of my trip, Mother and Daddy packed a suitcase and sack lunch and put me on a train bound for a two-day journey to what felt like the other side of the world. Just before I climbed on board, Daddy and Mother reminded me to mind my manners: Be polite. Don't ask for anything. Just wait. Mr. Murchison would get me a pillow and take me to the whites-only dining car for a meal before it opened or after it closed. With that, I climbed aboard and made my way to the last seat in the railcar for black passengers.

For hours at a time, I sat with my face pressed against the passenger window and watched as the brilliant sunshine faded into night. Excitement churned in me. My head was so full of thoughts that I could hardly sleep. What would the city look like? Where would we go? What would I see? Would I meet any movie stars?

Finally, the train pulled into New York's Penn Station, and I followed the flow of the crowd up the stairs. There, just inside, Aunt Juanita and Uncle Freddie were waiting. I felt like a real-life Alice in Wonderland as I stepped off the train into that vast space. I had landed in a different world, and the thrill of it rushed through me like a current. Penn Station was at least twice as big as the Little Rock station. Throngs of people scurried about in all directions, full of energy and purpose. My uncle and aunt greeted me warmly and ushered me through the station. My head snapped back and forth as I took in all the faces, hues, and languages mingling in one place. We whizzed by a couple of water fountains and public restrooms, one for men and another for women. That's when it struck me: There wasn't a WHITES ONLY sign anywhere in sight.

Outside, we climbed onto a bus headed to my aunt and uncle's apartment. It amazed me that we just plopped down wherever we pleased. Not once did the bus driver eye us in his rearview mirror and order us to the back of the bus when white people wanted a seat. This was the freedom up north I'd heard so much about. I could tell already that being colored seemed to mean something else up here. Here, colored men and women seemed to walk with their backs a bit straighter, their heads higher, as though they had as much right as anybody else to occupy this time and space. My parents had ingrained in me all my life that people of all races were equal in the eyes of God. Here, in New York, I was getting a glimpse of life through His divine lens.

Aunt Juanita and Uncle Freddie had three children of their own—Camille, who was five; Renata, two; and Michael, an infant. My aunt was a short, deep-brown-skinned woman with a happy disposition, always bubbly and sweet. She stayed home with us during the day while Uncle Freddie worked as a hospital lab technician. He was thinly built, with wavy black hair, and skin on the light side of honey. He was part Cape Verdean and spoke Portuguese and Italian. He patiently played my interpreter and tour guide as we cruised the streets of New York. The family lived in a three-bedroom apartment in a dark redbrick building on West Sixty-Second Street. The complex was among the city's first public housing units, built primarily for veterans returning from World War II. It was brand-new and wonderful, nothing like the crumbling urban tenements that still stand in most major cities today. From the bedroom window, I could look out and see across the Hudson River into New Jersey. Sometimes, on hot nights, I'd stand in front of the window to try to catch a breeze and watch the boats cruising down the river. The lights looked like stars, dotting the landscape.

We walked about four blocks to Central Park to picnic, visit the zoo, play ball, or ride our bikes. I spent most of my time on a concrete playground in the courtyard of the apartment complex. Aunt Juanita took us outside to play on the swings and jungle gym almost every day.

The summer of 1950 was full of firsts for me, grand and small. It was there that I heard for the first time my new friends ask for "soda" or "soda pop" instead of a "cold drink," which we said back home. I saw firemen open a fire hydrant and neighborhood kids dash through the blast of water in their clothes again and again under the fiery sun. Among my other New York firsts was pizza.

Little Rock didn't have pizza, but my friend Peggy, who had visited New York one summer with her grandmother, had told me all about it.

"Make sure you try the pizza," she reminded me constantly.

I couldn't wait to tell her that it was every bit as delicious as she had described.

I also marveled over the Rockettes, Ellis Island, and the Statue of Liberty. I even took the train to Harlem to spend the weekend with my great-uncle Callon Holloway (Uncle Buster). I felt like a real city slicker when I sat on the stoop with him and his friends at night, sometimes as late as midnight. They would set up a table and chairs under the streetlamp and gather around for games of dominoes, checkers, and cards, mostly pitty-pat. Uncle Buster took me to the Polo Grounds to see the Dodgers play the Giants, since he lived in Harlem. He was a Giants fan and I a Dodgers fan.

But among the more memorable experiences of that magical summer in New York were the times I spent with the white boy who became my best friend. His name was Francis. He had pale skin and strawberry-blond hair, and like me, he enjoyed playing stickball and tops. We met on the playground in the courtyard of Aunt Juanita's apartment complex, and from that day on, we played ball together, chased each other around the playground, and giggled over the silliest things. Most astonishing of all, no one even seemed to notice. I guess I took to him because he wasn't one of the most popular kids. And like me, he was an early bird, so we had plenty of energy to play ball in the morning. Francis and I weren't close enough to share secrets, like my friends Bunny, Peggy, and I did back home. There wasn't really anything all that extraordinary about my friendship with him, except this: Here in this brand-new world, an ordinary friendship between a little black girl and a little white boy could exist.

Summer zoomed by. Soon enough, my suitcases were packed and I was on the train, headed back to Little Rock, no longer the same girl. I'd tasted the sweetness of freedom and seen more than my eight-year-old mind could fully understand. But everything that the Jim Crow South had tried to make me believe about my people and my place in life had been flipped upside down. Suddenly, the world had opened wider. It was just a matter of time before I was ready to step out of the one I knew.

# CHAPTER 2

## The Playing Field

Softball was as much a summertime staple as home-made ice cream around my neighborhood. Practically every evening before sundown, a group of us gathered for a game, including my good friends Herbert Monts, Peggy Cyrus, Marion Davis, and Reba Davis and whoever else we could round up. If we collected fewer than ten people, we played in the street. But most days we rallied enough players for a real game—five or six members per team—and headed across Fifteenth Street to a huge vacant lot. It became our Ebbets Field—in more ways than one.

Just a few years after Jackie Robinson broke the color line in Major League Baseball at that historic New York stadium, a group of us schoolkids crossed that line, too, on a vacant lot in west Little Rock. Our motives were purely practical: The black kids needed more players to fill our teams. So we just began recruiting the white kids passing on their bikes.

"Want to join us?" one of us called out.

Before long, we had a group of regulars: J.R., Connie, Billy, Jay, and Pete. There wasn't a moment of trouble or awkwardness. Yet I was keenly aware that what was happening on our field was different. Aside from those three months in New York, I had never played with white kids before. I'd seen my white neighbors in passing, standing in their doorways, sitting on their porches, or riding their bikes along our roads. We usually acknowledged one another with a polite nod or even a "hello." But the division between us was clear.

Things were quite different among my black neighbors, which included a mix of professionals—a doctor, lawyer, college professor, and high school teacher—as well as postal, railroad, and construction workers, like my dad and his friend Sam Mumford. Mr. Mumford lived about a block away, and every morning he would walk to our house to meet Daddy. When I made it to the kitchen, Mr. Mumford would be sitting at the table with a cup of coffee and the newspaper. He always helped me with current events, especially when I got to junior high school. By then, I was taking civics and had to bring in a news topic for discussion.

"So, what's happening in the news today?" I'd ask.

Mr. Mumford would look up from the paper and

launch a discussion about whatever news had caught his attention that day. Thanks to him, I left home each morning feeling more prepared for class.

The neighborhood was full of kind people like Mr. Mumford. Even the families that didn't have children my age welcomed us into their homes. I especially liked spending time with a neighborhood couple, A. B. and Doll Fox, who were in their fifties and lived across Fifteenth Street, next to the field. They were the surrogate grandparents of the neighborhood, the first to stop over with home-cooked food if someone was sick, and the first to offer hugs and help if misfortune struck one of the families. They were the ones who somehow managed to stay connected to everybody's lives. I watched boxing matches with Mr. Fox, an industrial arts teacher and real Renaissance man, who also played the cello. Some of our neighbors called him "Professor." He was too humble to accept the name. But the title fit him perfectly. Mr. Fox was a smart man and by nature philosophical. He was always teaching, even when we didn't realize in the moment exactly what we were being taught. As I was about to enter junior high school, Mr. Fox warned: Always be prepared because you will be tested every day.

The thought at first intimidated me because I thought he was talking about written tests. But more conversations with him revealed that he was sharing a deeper lesson about life and making good decisions. His wife, Doll, loved to bake, and she kept homemade goodies around their house. She knew my father had a huge sweet tooth, so she usually sent me home with slices of pound cake or sweet-potato pie for him.

Our neighborhood was full of kids about the same age, and the black parents saw it as their moral duty to keep watch over us all, correct us, and, if necessary, report any misbehavior to one another. While my parents were generally mild-mannered folks who rarely raised their voices, I knew that nothing could result in serious trouble at home quicker than embarrassing them or bringing shame to the Walls name by acting up in public. The black kids rode bikes, walked to the corner store, and swam together in the segregated swimming pool at Gilliam Park, a small recreational area operated by the city for Little Rock's black residents. We also knew and respected one another's parents as our own. But when it came to our white playmates, we knew nothing more than their first names.

On our softball playing field, though, everything was level. Our teams were integrated, and every one of us played hard. For the most part, we also played fair. We knew how one another hit, caught, and ran. We knew who played dirty and who could steal a base. And none of us was above boasting when the game ended in our favor.

"We'll whip you again tomorrow," I proclaimed many times after victory.

I imagined myself as Jackie Robinson and always played first or second base. I was somewhat tomboyish and one of the better players. I also was usually among the first ones picked for a team. In those moments on that field, there was no black or white, just winners and losers and kids being kids.

Away from the field, though, the boundaries were clear and unspoken. Of course, at that time in the Jim Crow South, there were limited places for black and white children to socialize together. We black kids weren't allowed at the same public parks, swimming pools, restaurants, movie theater rows, or even water fountains. And we went to Stephens Elementary School.

In my early days there, Stephens was an old, multistory building that sat atop the hill on West Eighteenth Street. Big wood-burning stoves in each room provided heat in the winter, and we relied on big fans to keep the rooms cool in early summer. But the old building was replaced a couple of years after I arrived, by a more modern, one-story building. From as early as I can remember, I walked up that hill every day alone or with other schoolmates to class. Parents felt safe enough to let us go.

I was a sixth grader at Stephens in May 1954 when news about the historic *Brown v. Board of Education* broke. I read about it in the *Weekly Reader,* a popular children's newspaper. My teacher, Mrs. King, explained that the highest court in the land had decided it was unfair and against the law for black and white children to attend separate schools. Black children would finally have access to the same opportunities the white students had, she told us. Being a kid, I thought she meant we'd see some changes—new books, at least—right away. I was disappointed when, as far as I could tell, nothing changed that year. The next year, I moved to the all-black Paul Laurence Dunbar Junior and Senior High School, which had been named for the internationally renowned black poet.

Some days, I caught a ride with a family member or rode the city bus to school. But most of the time, I walked the two-plus miles. I'd pass Roselawn Cemetery and cross the bridge over the Union Pacific Railroad track. Then, there it was—to my left, just one mile from my house, the all-white Little Rock Central High School. That grand school building, with a campus that spread across four square blocks, loomed just beyond in the distance. Its stadium was so close that on Friday and Saturday evenings during football season, I could see the bright lights shining from Central's football field in the neighborhood.

But the school's reputation extended far beyond its championship football teams and sports facilities. The school had a stellar reputation for sending its graduates to the top-rated colleges in the country, often on scholarships, Mr. Fox told me. It also had a huge two-thousand-seat auditorium, professional stage, and state-of-the-art lighting for students interested in theater. Students interested in biology and science had access to a fully equipped greenhouse.

Sometimes, as I passed Central, I wondered what it would be like to be a student there and have access to all that and more. I was a serious student who made As and Bs and spent a good bit of time thinking about my future. I had recently begun dreaming of becoming a doctor after reading about Madame Curie, the first woman in France to receive a doctorate, and the only woman to receive the Nobel Prize twice. She was a brilliant scientist whose discoveries in the field of radiation changed the world. I liked that her discoveries helped prove to the world the scientific capabilities of women. I didn't know of any women doctors and certainly not any black ones, but Madame Curie had inspired me to take a chance. I loved science, and I liked the idea of helping people, of changing the world. I was sure that Central would have everything I needed to reach those goals someday. Maybe there, I thought, I could even get a new biology or chemistry book—one that I could write my name in. At Dunbar, all my books were hand-me-downs from the white schools. By the time I got them, a white kid's name was already scrawled across the front cover. Some of the books were so shabby and worn that they were missing pages.

I frequently heard complaints about the outdated

textbooks, limited supplies, and inferior equipment at the black schools from the relatives and family friends who worked there. Practically everywhere I turned at Dunbar, I was under the watchful eye of an aunt, uncle, or family friend who was on staff. Among them were my Aunt Eva, the librarian; Uncle Silas, who taught auto mechanics; and my neighbor Mr. Fox. My seventh-grade gym teacher also became my aunt Whaletha when she married my mother's brother, Med Jr., the summer after I took her class. I'd hear the adults talking among themselves about the injustice of it all, with white schools always getting the best of everything.

The disparities between Dunbar and Central can be traced to their beginnings. In 1927, the Little Rock school district spent $1.5 million to build what would become Little Rock Central High School. News reports called the school the most expensive high school in the nation. Little money was left to build a school for black children until some private financing came in. Dunbar was built by some tax dollars and mostly by Rosenwald Funds. Dunbar is considered a Rosenwald School.

The architecture of the schools look quite similar, each with columns and concrete steps. But the schools have always been far from equal. Central, with one hundred classrooms spread across six hundred thousand square feet, served as a senior high school and junior college. Meanwhile, Dunbar, with thirty-four classrooms spread over two hundred thousand square feet, operated as a junior high, senior high, and junior college. Central's first library had over twice as many books as Dunbar's. Central had both a gymnasium and a stadium, but Dunbar had neither until 1950, when a gym was added. The boys and girls basketball teams practiced and played at large halls or centers located in the black community, like the YMCA.

Despite the discrepancies, though, Dunbar was far more modern than the one-room shacks where black children were forced to be educated throughout much of the South. Its deeply intelligent all-black staff helped to create an academically rigorous curriculum. Many of Dunbar's teachers had advanced degrees and often spent their summers taking classes at northern universities. What they lacked in resources, they made up for in creativity and dedication. Educating black children was more than a job back then; it was a mission—one that was rooted in the teachings of historically black colleges and universities—like Philander Smith College or Howard University. These schools had been created in the wake of the Civil War to educate formerly enslaved black folks—and they instilled in their students a duty to give back to their community. In that spirit, the Dunbar staff pushed us to excel.

My biology teacher, Edna Douglas, was one of my favorites. She had taught Mother, and she was a worldly woman who had traveled far and wide. She wove stories of her travels into her lectures and left us captivated with her descriptions of the people and places she had seen. Mrs. Douglas did more than teach science. She took us to those faraway places and made them more than just dots on a map. She engaged me in the world beyond Little Rock and made me want to see more of it. A good education was the door to the broader world, she told her students.

Dunbar's reputation as a top-notch school attracted black students from all over Arkansas, who stayed with relatives to attend. Some were from well-to-do families who wanted their children to have access to the best possible education. Others were from rural areas that had no schools for black children. Not only did my parents graduate from Dunbar's high school, but Mother also graduated from the junior college. After World War II, Daddy spent a year at the junior college on the GI Bill as well. They never lost their tremendous affection for their alma mater.

I, too, have fond memories of Dunbar. I was an honor student and captain of the girls basketball team, a class representative on the student council, a member of the Junior National Honor Society, captain of the cheerleading squad, and a member of the choir. I also served as vice president of the student council two years in a row. In my day, girls were never selected to be president of the council.

I was in the seventh grade at Dunbar when the school district announced plans to build two new high schools, Horace Mann for black students and Hall High for whites. When the new high schools opened in fall 1956, Dunbar was to convert exclusively to a junior high school. Word of the new black high school circulated quickly among my junior high school peers. We were excited about it. I didn't realize then that the new schools were part of an overall plan to respond to the Supreme Court decision that I had read about the previous year in the *Weekly Reader.*

The school system's plan hailed a new era. Now the process of desegregating schools could begin. It would start with a small number of black students entering Central High School in the fall of 1957. In the following years, other black students would enter all-white junior high and elementary schools. The proposal would come to be known as the Blossom Plan, named for Virgil T. Blossom, superintendent of Little Rock public schools.

But the school system wasn't enthusiastic in the least and would fiercely refuse to cooperate with the plan. In fact, as one school board member suggested, the plan would provide "as little integration as possible for as long as legally possible." Horace Mann would be built on one side of town and be all black. Hall High, in an affluent white area, would not admit any black students. That left Central, which was surrounded by working-class white and racially mixed neighborhoods. It would become the first testing ground for school integration in the city.

I watched Horace Mann rise slowly from the dirt when my friends and I headed to Gilliam Park to swim during the summer of 1955. In a few years, I'll be a student there, I thought to myself. But high school was on the back burner. I was just looking forward to returning to Dunbar for eighth grade. In August of that summer, though, a brutal crime nearly two hundred miles away in Money, Mississippi, rattled me to the core.

I first heard the name of Emmett Till whispered from the lips of adults, speaking in hushed tones around my house about the horrible thing the white people did to that little black boy in Mississippi. My parents subscribed to the *Chicago Defender,* that city's black newspaper, and it was there that I first read the full, terrifying story. As I followed the story for weeks in the black press, I couldn't get the images out of my head. How Till, a fourteen-year-old Chicago boy visiting his great-uncle in Money, Mississippi, walked to white-owned Bryant's Grocery on August 24, 1955, with some friends after a long day in the cotton fields. How the teenager, unfamiliar with the deadly taboos of the South, may have whistled at a white woman while leaving the store. How Roy Bryant, the store owner and the white woman's husband, showed up with his half brother four days later at the home where Till was staying and dragged him away. How Till's battered and mutilated body was pulled from the Tallahatchie River a few days later. How the body had been weighed down by a seventy-five-pound cotton gin fan attached by barbed wire.

As horrible as those images were in my imagination, nothing could have prepared me for the real-life pictures I saw when Mother's September 15, 1955, issue of *Jet* magazine arrived at our home. As I flipped open the magazine and turned to the story about Emmett Till's memorial service, I gasped. The photo of his badly disfigured corpse was right there, in black and white. Part of me was so horrified that I wanted to turn the page quickly or throw the magazine down, but I couldn't take my eyes off his bloated, monstrous face. It was one of those moments when legend meets reality.

I had read stories before about the lynching of black folks in Mississippi and other areas of the Deep South. I'd even heard my relatives tell the story of a lynching in downtown Little Rock. A woman who appeared to be in her early forties sat on her porch about five blocks from my home every day, just staring at passersby through sad, empty eyes. Her mind was never quite right, my folks said, because her brother had been lynched on Broadway when she was still in her mother's womb. To me, such stories were tragic yet distant history. But I *knew* Emmett Till. I'd never laid eyes on him before the magazine photos, but in the handsome face of the boy he had been before his murder, I saw my cousins, my friends, my classmates. He was just one and a half years older than me and as real to me as the black playmates I met on the softball field every day.

Emmett's death said to me that for a black child, a little too much confidence, a joke, saying or doing the wrong thing, in the wrong place, at the wrong time, or just being the wrong color could cost him his life. And it horrified me.

Because of what happened to Emmett Till, Mississippi became a fearsome place in my mind, and I wanted never to set foot there. That must have been the case with the adults in my family, too, because from that moment on, Daddy mapped out our road trips so that we never even passed through Mississippi. Those were the days before the interstate highway system, and sometimes we might have gotten to our destination quicker by going through Mississippi. But we weren't taking any chances.

Somehow, though, I still did not see Little Rock through the same eyes as I saw Mississippi. Yes, Little Rock was the South. Yes, I had to sit in the back of the bus and climb to the black section in the balcony when Peggy, Reba, and I walked to the Lee Theater for a movie. Yes, I'd heard white folks make degrading comments. Yes,

I knew I couldn't swim at the nearby War Memorial Park (formerly Fair Park), because the pool was for whites only. Yet in my mind, my hometown was not as bad as Mississippi. Till's murder had set the bar for racial evil in my mind, and compared with that, Little Rock wasn't too bad—or so I thought. At that point, I had always played by the rules. I'd never stepped out of my so-called place. That would come a few years later, and I would be shocked and saddened to see my hometown for the first time as it really was.

In fact, black residents in Little Rock were growing restless from being treated like second-class citizens. At the end of 1955, the black solidarity taking place in Montgomery, Alabama, was making headlines—and the black residents of Arkansas were feeling empowered by it.

I had felt such pride reading about how the black people of Montgomery were refusing to ride public buses, to protest the segregation and racism they faced on them. I eagerly followed the news and photos of the Montgomery bus boycott in black newspapers and magazines, showing how fifty thousand black men and women there were working together, walking and carpooling to work, church, and everywhere else they had to go, while empty buses crisscrossed the city. I knew the whole story—how a small act of defiance by Rosa Parks had ignited the boycott. What a gracious lady. I imagined that she was just bone-tired that day when she quietly refused a white bus driver's order that she give up her seat to a white passenger. I had sat on the bus next to many black women like her in Little Rock. They would be headed home from jobs cleaning, cooking, and sewing in white people's homes and businesses all day, so tired they could barely keep their eyes open. When I saw that iconic black-and-white photograph of Rosa Parks being fingerprinted after her arrest for taking such a bold stand, I thought of all the hardworking women she had uplifted by keeping her seat. And she became my forever shero.

I recognized the infectious power of the Montgomery movement one day in early 1956 when my cousin Delores and I decided to ride the bus downtown. As we stepped on board, we noticed Alexine Duncan, one of the granddaughters of the older couple who lived across the street from me. Alexine was in her twenties and had spent some time in Denver, Colorado, where her father operated an upscale men's clothing store. Like me, she had traveled up north and lived another way. Delores and I waved hello and we sat across from her in the middle of the bus, where the black section began. The bus grew more and more crowded as it traveled down Park Avenue. Suddenly, at one stop, a white passenger boarded, and the driver looked up into his rearview mirror at Delores and me and shouted over his shoulder:

"You two girls, get up!"

We knew he meant for us to go to the back and clear

that row for white passengers. Without question, we were about to comply when I heard a sharp reply from across the aisle:

"Oh, no, you don't! You stay right there!"

Delores and I froze in our tracks and looked up. It was Alexine. She was fuming. Her arms were folded across her chest, and she was staring the bus driver down. We had a right to sit there, she announced. Hadn't he heard about the Montgomery bus boycotts?

I knew that Alexine was probably thinking of Rosa Parks and feeling the call of history to take her own stand. But as she grew louder, refusing to back down even after the bus driver threatened to call the police, I grew more frightened. I wanted to disappear. I wanted to run off the bus. I've never been the kind of person to make a scene, and that was the last thing I wanted right then.

But it was too late.

The next thing I knew, the police were climbing aboard to escort Alexine off the bus. Delores and I got off, too, and quietly walked back home.

I never talked to Alexine about what happened that day, but I always felt horrible that she had landed in the hands of the police for standing up for me on that bus. Little did I know that another integration battle was heating up in my hometown. And soon, I would take my own stand.

# CHAPTER 3

## A New Era

By the spring of 1957, my days at Dunbar were winding down. Ninth grade was almost over, and high school was just around the corner. The idea of going to the brand-new Horace Mann had grown on me. I looked forward to moving with my friends there. Just the idea of attending a school where everything was new—the building, the classrooms, the labs, the lockers—was exciting.

Then one day before the end of the school year, my homeroom teacher made an announcement: Central High School would be integrating in the fall. If our homes fell within certain border streets and we were interested in attending, we should sign the sheet of paper circulating around the classroom. Three years after the U.S. Supreme Court had ordered schools to integrate, it was really about to happen in Little Rock. But you wouldn't have known there was anything special about this moment. No one asked a question, commented, or even whispered. If there was any excitement, uncertainty, nervousness, or fear in the room, none of my peers or our teacher expressed it.

It caught my attention, though. My address did put me in Central's attendance zone. I had a quick decision to make. My mind weighed the options. Central High, that grand building looming in the distance as I walked to school practically every day, now would open its doors to me. I'd heard so much about it. I knew I could get into the historically black colleges Philander Smith or Arkansas AM&N—yet I couldn't help wondering how much wider my college options would be if I attended Central and suddenly had all its resources available to me. Plus, Central had competitive athletic teams, and it was just a mile from my home, much closer than Mann. My decision was made. When the sign-up sheet got to me, I eagerly wrote down my name.

When I made it home from school that afternoon, I didn't even mention my decision to my parents. It wasn't a calculated choice to keep the news from them. It just never came up. I know that sounds strange, but I've always been independent. I also tend not to make a big deal of things, even at times when something really is a big deal. In my mind, I had done what my parents would have expected. They had told me all my life that a good education was essential and that I should always strive for better. Central seemed the better choice for me, so my decision didn't stick out in my mind as one that needed much discussion. I must say, though, I was also just naive. I thought I had made a simple decision to go to a different school. I had no idea how much my life and the lives of those closest to me were about to change.

As the school year ended, my thoughts turned to summer. I knew the Brooklyn Dodgers would play the Cardinals and that my family would drive to St. Louis for the game. By then, Daddy also had bought our first television so we could see some games from home, too.

These were good financial times. Construction jobs were plentiful, and for several years, Daddy had been earning enough money to splurge on a few luxuries, like the TV. He also was putting the finishing touches on a new wing he had added onto the back of the house, including a new den and a large master bedroom for my parents. The room was spacious and bright, with lots of light streaming in the windows. Among my favorite features of the room were its oak hardwood floors, which I had helped Daddy lay.

Daddy taught me lots of practical skills, including some tasks that fathers of my generation were more likely to teach their sons. I helped out when he mowed the yard and trimmed the bushes. He would even have me watch while he changed a tire on the car. When he worked in Big Daddy's café, I set up tables and delivered orders to the cook. He taught me how to make chili mac (home-made chili with macaroni or spaghetti added), one of the mainstays at the café. And when he worked the cash register, I sat on a high stool while he showed me again and again how to count money and give change to customers quickly. I was just thirteen when he first taught me to drive. He and I would hop into his truck and head to a deserted back road somewhere in town, then he'd hand over the wheel. Daddy was a patient and diligent teacher, always had been, ever since I'd been a toddler and he taught me my ABCs and numbers.

My teenage friends were crazy about Daddy, too, especially the guys, some of whom found it difficult to communicate with their own fathers, who tended to be more rigid and stern. Herbert Monts, one of the regulars in our neighborhood softball games, once told me that he always enjoyed talking to my father. He said that Daddy was playful and down-to-earth, that Daddy really listened and never talked down to him.

Daddy had a big soft spot in his heart for his daughters. Mother did, too. Nothing revealed that more than when the two of them decided during the summer to give their dream bedroom to me. They hadn't even moved in yet when they surprised me with the news. Now that I was going to high school, they told me, I would need a quiet place to study. I could hardly believe my ears. For the first time in my life, I had a room of my own. I knew how much my parents wanted and needed a bigger bed-room, but they were willing to wait at least a few more years until I left for college. Their sacrifice and generosity spoke eloquently to me about what they considered im-portant: My education meant far more to them than their own desire for comfort.

When it came to taste and style, my parents were two of a kind. They didn't have much, but whenever they pulled themselves together for a night on the town, they looked like a million bucks—Daddy in his Italian-designed hat, dress suit, and shoes, and Mother in something flowing, with glittery jewels around her neck. There was nothing pretentious or haughty about Mother. Daddy just loved spoiling her. He often worked two or three jobs at a time, whatever it took to provide for his family. His family was his pride. You could see it all over his face, especially when he stepped out with his glamorous wife on his arm.

That sense of style extended to our home. As my par-ents made changes here and there, our house took on a modern look, inspired—I'm almost certain—by Mother's many magazines, including *Life,* as well as *Ebony* and *Sepia,* which were black-owned publications focused pri-marily on black success. They particularly showcased the glitz and glamour of the few black movie stars and enter-tainers of the time.

Mother's touch was noticeable everywhere that sum-mer as she finished the transformation of our house, bringing in new, lovely furniture. I spent many evenings curled up in the white leather swivel chair in front of the television. For the expanded kitchen, my parents added a bar with red-padded chrome stools. When I plopped down many mornings on those barstools with my piping hot grits and scrambled eggs, I felt as if I were in one of those California diners I'd seen on television.

Daddy was a prankster who kept us all laughing. But he was wise, too, and very much the traditional head of our household. I didn't see families that looked like mine—happy black families—on TV, but we were a stable clan with loving, doting parents. Daddy worked, Mother primarily took care of the family's domestic needs, and we children got to be just children. Our home was peaceful, full of laughter, and often full of extended family. Some of my favorite family times were spent in front of that black-and-white television, watching a broadcast of a Dodgers game. On those Saturdays, we'd gather in the den with friends and my uncles and their wives or girlfriends. I'd cook hamburgers, while my sister Loujuana, then eight, played with her dolls. All the while, my two-year-old sister, Tina, ran from one family member's lap to another.

That summer, as I had every June and July, I sold bags of potato chips to raise money for Y-Teen camp, a two-week program sponsored by the local YWCA. And I must say, I was pretty good at it. I hiked through the neighborhood, to church, to family gatherings with my chips in tow. Going to camp motivated me to sell them all. I loved camp. It was two weeks of freedom with some really good friends. My best friend, Bunny, always joined me. Her real name is Dorothy Frazier, and we've been friends for as long as I can remember. Her grandmother lived just a block away from my house and across the street from the church we attended. Bunny's father had died in World War II when she was a baby, and she lived with her mother and stepfather, who was a doctor.

I also enjoyed spending time at camp with another good friend, Jeannette Mazique, who lived in another city in Arkansas. Jeannette and I had met through our fathers, who sometimes worked construction jobs together. Because we lived far away, we didn't get to see each other much until camp.

Bunny, Jeannette, and I rode the bus with the other Y-Teens to Camp Clearfork, just outside Hot Springs. I didn't realize then that it was the only site in our area that admitted black campers. It was beautiful and serene, several acres of woods surrounding a sparkling lake. Rustic cabins sat nestled among the trees. We rose early most mornings to hike, compete in games, and participate in arts and crafts projects, like making key chains. At night, we enjoyed cooking out and singing around an open campfire. I could hardly wait.

But camp was at the end of July, still a few weeks away. In the meantime, I spent my days at the nearby Dunbar

Community Center, a gathering place for black Little Rock. Something fun was always happening there. In the evenings and on weekends, black fraternities, sororities, and other groups held meetings and parties in the center's huge hall on the main level. A smaller room upstairs drew families and church groups for afternoon receptions. But during the day, the center belonged to the city's kids. It was always full of children and teens, playing games and cards while the latest sounds of rock and roll blared from the jukebox—Chuck Berry, Little Richard, Elvis Presley, Fats Domino, you name it. One afternoon, I was headed inside when I spotted Ernest Green, a friend and former Dunbar student. Ernie was two years older and about to enter his senior year. His mother had been my first-grade teacher. The two of us greeted each other, chatted for a moment, and then he asked:

"Are you going to Central?"

"Yep," I responded proudly.

He told me that he had signed up, too, but that none of his friends wanted to leave Mann in their senior year. Ernie asked if I knew of anyone else who had signed up, but I didn't. My friend Peggy, who lived two blocks from me, had told me she had no interest in going to Central. She was having too much fun at the new Mann.

Ernie looked concerned. "We need to contact a few people and see if they want to go with us," he said.

We agreed.

"See you at Central," I said.

A few weeks later, I stepped outside my home to meet the postman, as usual, and was surprised to find a letter for me from the Little Rock school district. I read it quickly and ran inside to show Mother confirmation of my admittance to Central. She smiled and congratulated me. That's the first time I remember any communication with her about my decision to go to Central. There was no big discussion, but I could tell she was happy for me. The card instructed me to show up at Central on a certain date in August to register for fall classes. Now I was getting excited.

But just two days into August, misfortune struck my family.

I was standing on the porch that day when Mother stepped to the front door and called me inside. The distress on her face and her red eyes told me right away that something was wrong. Papa Holloway was gone, she said. Our patriarch—the man who had raised her, protected her, and kept the ground beneath her steady in those early days after her mother left—was dead. My aunt Helen had found him unconscious, lying among the corn in his expansive garden. I hugged her as she wept inconsolably. My heart ached, too.

Papa's death dulled the excitement I had felt in the

days before. But as relatives chatted in our home after the funeral on August 7, I heard Mother tell some out-of-town relatives:

"You know, Carlotta will be going to Central in the fall."

There was pride in her voice, which lifted my spirits.

However, when word got out that I was going to Central, not everyone in my family agreed with my decision. I couldn't understand why Aunt Eva, the Dunbar librarian, didn't seem particularly excited when I told her. That was unusual for her because she was such an upbeat, fun-loving person. I'd learn through the family grapevine much later that she wanted my parents to withdraw me from Central and send me to Mann. She didn't understand why I needed to go to "that school."

Aunt Eva and all the other staff members at Dunbar were a proud bunch, and rightly so. They had given up their summers and holidays to add postgraduate degrees to their résumés. They had labored in a school system that still paid them less than a less-educated white teacher. They had invested their skills and hearts in preparing black children for a world that would demand them to be twice as good and work twice as hard. And they had produced stellar students, despite the imbalance in resources. But they weren't at all confident that their white colleagues at Central would be able to look past the skin color of black students, or see and nurture the future doctors, lawyers, and scientists we could become.

As a stubbornly determined teenager, I couldn't fully understand why all my relatives weren't thrilled that I was preparing to attend one of the top high schools in America. Hadn't they always preached to me about the value of education and opportunity?

Now I understand their concerns. But at the time, I just tuned them out. So as registration day grew closer, I called Gloria Ray, a classmate at Dunbar. We had taken typing together and were members of the Honor Society. She was a serious student—she wanted to be an atomic scientist, for goodness' sake. I suspected that if anyone else was considering Central, she was on the list. I was right. Gloria told me that she was indeed planning to attend and had received the same card about registration day. She agreed to pick me up.

As planned, Gloria and I rode together to Central for the first time. We considered the day so routine that we went without our parents. Our parents were very protective and would have demanded to go along if they'd had any inkling of trouble, particularly Gloria's father, who was much older than my parents. And Gloria was the baby of their family.

She parked the car about a block away from Central, and we made our way to the front of the school. It was a clear, sunny day, and as we moved closer, I was filled with awe. I had never been this close to the front of Central before, and the yellowish brick and white concrete building was even bigger and more elegant than I had imagined. As I stared up at that great entrance, I felt tiny. Gloria and I climbed the steps, headed for the main entrance on the second floor. At the top, we passed beneath four white, life-size statues of Greek gods and goddesses. Each bore an inscription that seemed to carry a message about the place: AMBITION, PERSONALITY, OPPORTUNITY, PREPARATION.

At first, when Gloria and I stepped inside the school, we didn't know which way to go. Signs pointed toward the main office to our left, so we went that way. We had barely made it inside when a woman behind the counter quickly rose from her seat and approached us. I announced that we were there to register for the fall semester. She introduced herself as the school's registrar. She handed each of us a card that said we had to attend a special meeting at Superintendent Blossom's office with our parents before we could register. Gloria and I looked at each other, completely baffled. The woman was firm, not the warm and fuzzy type, but pleasant enough as she explained that everything would be okay; the superintendent just needed to meet with us and our parents. None of the other administrative workers even looked our way. Gloria and I thanked her and left.

We weren't quite sure what to make of what had just

happened. School officials had instructed us to show up for registration, only to give us another card requiring us to attend another meeting? Why did we need to meet with the superintendent, anyway? Why was it necessary to bring our parents? And who else would be at the meeting? Gloria and I grumbled all the way to the car.

As we got closer, we noticed a car parking just behind Gloria's car. An attractive, honey-colored woman wearing a dress and heels hopped out and hailed us over to her. I recognized her right away. It was Daisy Bates, president of the Arkansas State Conference of the NAACP (National Association for the Advancement of Colored People) branches. She and her husband, L. C. Bates, co-owned and -operated the *Arkansas State Press,* the black newspaper I had delivered on my paper route in elementary and junior high school. Mother worked occasionally as an NAACP volunteer. Mrs. Bates and Mother got along well. They were both pretty, ladylike southern women who placed great value in their manner and appearance. But where Mother was soft-spoken and quiet, Mrs. Bates was outspoken and opinionated. And in L. C. Bates, a longtime newspaperman, Daisy Bates had found a partner to take a stand for civil rights and to rally against police brutality, the mistreatment of black war veterans in the city, and other injustices against black residents.

Mrs. Bates greeted Gloria and me and immediately began asking questions about what had happened in the school. She wanted to know all the details—whom we saw, what had been said, how we were treated, whether we were allowed to register. We told her about the upcoming meeting with Superintendent Blossom and showed her the card.

That was the beginning of my almost daily contact with the woman who soon became an adviser, mentor, and biggest public defender.

I didn't question why Mrs. Bates had come to meet us at the school or even how she knew Gloria and I would be there. It would have been impolite to ask. The way I was raised, children stayed in their place, and it was not my place to ask a woman of her authority why she was there and whether she was expecting trouble.

At fourteen, I was old enough to understand the historical significance of my enrollment in Central and the NAACP's interest in it. It was the NAACP and its brilliant attorneys, after all, who had fought for the ruling in the *Brown v. Board of Education* case in the first place. I also knew some white folks wouldn't like the idea of black students going to Central. But I really believed that what the U.S. Supreme Court said should happen *would* happen because it was now the law of the land.

I believed, too, that my presence at Central would allow my white peers to see that beyond the color of our skin, we all wanted the same thing: a fun and unforgettable high school experience, the best education possible, a jump start for our futures. I had no clue that while I was counting down the days until I started my new school, enraged white parents and other citizens—including the Arkansas governor, who had gotten my parents' vote in the last election—were organizing to keep me away.

I'd been too caught up with the events of summer to pay much attention to the local newspapers, which were full of stories about the activities of the Capital Citizens' Council and the Mothers' League. Both groups were organizing to stop the integration of Central, and pushing Governor Orval Faubus for a delay in implementing the Blossom Plan. A poll even indicated that 85 percent of the white population in Little Rock opposed school integration. Many threatened violence if black students were allowed to enter Central.

One of the most vocal segregationists was Reverend James Wesley Pruden, the pastor of Broadmoor Baptist Church and a member of the anti-integration Citizens' Council. He ran newspaper ads to help whip up the public frenzy. The ads asked questions that seemed to reveal the underlying source of all the fear: Would black boys and white girls be allowed to dance together at school dances? Would black boys and white girls be paired in romantic love scenes in school plays? The mere thought that their white daughters would be in such proximity to black boys petrified white mothers and fathers throughout Little Rock.

Mother and I left home early that August evening to make sure we made it on time to the meeting in Blossom's downtown office. By the time the meeting began, about thirty-nine students and our parents were crammed shoulder to shoulder in the small space.

I felt a bit anxious, unsure why we were all there. What was there to discuss? Hadn't the Supreme Court said that black students should have the same educational opportunities as our white peers? Central was my neighborhood school, and I'd made my choice. I knew I was a good enough student to make it there. I looked at Superintendent Blossom, who sat stoically behind a large wooden desk. He was a big, tall, white man with dark hair slicked back lightly and a pair of black glasses perched on his nose. Blossom's serious expression didn't change when he started to speak. He had called us there to go over the rules, he explained. Black students would be allowed to attend Central, as expected, he said, but it would take time on both sides to adjust. We might hear some name-calling, but we were not to retaliate in any way. For our own safety, he added, we had to leave the school grounds as soon as our classes ended. That meant we would not be allowed to participate in any extracurricular activities—no varsity sports, clubs, chorus, band, or even the Student Government Association. We also could not attend any after-school parties or sporting events.

Central had a championship team whose winning

streak had lasted over a year, and I'd been looking forward to attending the games. I could just imagine myself with my classmates in the stands in Central's college-size football stadium, cheering with school spirit and pride.

Blossom could not be serious, I thought. I'd always maintained a full roster of extracurricular activities. That was the fun part of school. My family encouraged my getting involved. It helped to make me well-rounded, they said. Now I was expected to give up all of it? What about baseball and basketball? What about cheerleading, the student council, and the National Honor Society? Wouldn't those kinds of activities give black and white students a chance to work together and get to know one another? The superintendent had no idea how involved I had been at my old school or how good I was at sports, I thought. When my white classmates got to know me, when they saw me play, they would want me to join their organizations and athletic teams. I was sure of it. So part of me just tuned Superintendent Blossom out. In my mind, this was simply a formality. Blossom was saying what he believed he had to say. But I was certain things would be much different when I got to Central.

Sitting in that room taking it all in, I was still under the impression that the decision to attend Central High School had been all mine. That I'd sealed the deal when I signed the sheet of paper in my homeroom class at Dunbar. I had no idea that Little Rock school officials had been given the biggest say. That *they* had approved me. I would learn decades later that by the time we black students showed up at Blossom's office, every one of us had been thoroughly vetted. So Blossom knew exactly what kind of student I had been at Dunbar. I imagine that I, as well as all the others in the room that day, were not just the best and brightest students academically, but we were student leaders from working- and middle-class families whose backgrounds had been deemed "acceptable" by the school system's white leaders.

I snapped out of my own little world when I heard Blossom specifically address the boys in the room. The room was full of black teenage boys listening intently as the superintendent put them on notice:

"You are not to date—or even look at—our girls," he said.

I distinctly remember his using the word *our*. The girls weren't just white; they were his. They were special. I was stunned. What did that have to do with anything? I thought about my friend Ernie. I also thought for a moment about Emmett Till. I wondered how Ernie and the other guys in the room must have felt. What if they accidentally bumped into a white girl? Or, God forbid, smiled at one? Would it be misinterpreted? Would they be reprimanded? Or worse?

Everyone else must have been shocked, too, because no one said a word. The room was so still, it felt as though no one even breathed. There were no questions or discussion. Even as parents and their children filed out of the room, there was silence, uneasiness.

Mother and I walked quietly to the car. I slowed my stride. Mother wouldn't dare let me know if she was concerned about what she had just heard. She would wait and talk it over with Daddy behind closed doors. I knew that if they felt too worried, they could just put their foot down and say I couldn't go to Central after all. As independent as I was, I had no illusions about who was in charge. I knew I would just have to wait to find out where my parents stood.

On the drive home, Mother wore her usual composed look. She always did, even in the midst of trouble. But from the time I was a child, I've always been able to see right through her. I learned early to read her eyes. They always told me the truth, even when her behavior or her words did not. And that evening, her eyes told me something was wrong. She was worried. This was not going to be an ordinary school year. Blossom certainly had made that clear.

But if Blossom had intended to change my mind, it didn't work. Even the worry in Mother's eyes didn't give me a second thought about my decision. I was as determined as ever to go to Central.

# CHAPTER 4

## Wait and See

Just before Labor Day, my great-uncle Emerald Holloway stopped by the house with a surprise gift for me: cash to buy a brand-new outfit for my first day at Central. Everybody in the family knew that Mother was a terrific seamstress who usually made all my clothes. But this was no ordinary first day of school, Uncle Em said. The integration of the finest high school in Arkansas would happen just once in our lifetime, and I needed a dress to match the occasion.

Mother and I took the bus downtown and searched our favorite department stores until we found the perfect outfit: a black skirt set with small, bluish-green letters and numbers spread in a random pattern. The blouse had short sleeves, just right for the hot and humid early days of September, and the skirt was pleated at the waist. The outfit looked sophisticated and smart, not too dainty. I hung the skirt set in my closet to wait for the big day: September 3, the Tuesday after Labor Day.

Labor Day marked the end of summer vacation, and my family spent the afternoon at Gilliam Park. The pool was so full of people that you could barely swim a clear path from one side to the other. My family cooked hot dogs and hamburgers in the grassy picnic area. Teenagers danced to the rhythm and blues and rock and roll blaring from the intercom. About midday, I heard a rumor that Governor Faubus would appear on late-night television news to make a speech about Central.

I was having too much fun to give it much thought. My parents didn't seem worried either. They liked Governor Faubus. They had voted for him twice before in previous elections. He was a man of the people, I'd heard them say, and not a segregationist. He certainly was no John Patterson, the Alabama governor who had banned the NAACP from operating in his state and welcomed the support of the Ku Klux Klan. And neither was Governor Faubus a Marvin Griffin, the brash Georgia governor who promised to keep the schools in his state segregated "come hell or high water."

Yet what we hadn't known was that Governor Faubus had spent the summer cavorting with well-known segregationists—and that he had very much come around to their ways.

That night, after a day of swimming and barbecuing,

my family gathered in front of the television in the den at ten p.m. to watch the news. None of us expected anything earth-shattering. This was my bedtime, and quite frankly, I was just eager to get to sleep so I could be well rested for my first day of school the next day.

About fifteen minutes after the hour, Governor Faubus appeared on-screen. Like Blossom, he was a big man. He wore a dark suit and tie and spoke with a southern drawl. I listened as he droned on the first few minutes about the history of race relations in Arkansas. But at age fourteen, I found it hard to sit still for long periods, especially during rambling speeches. I was about to start daydreaming when the governor said something that caught my attention:

> Before the forcible integration of Negroes and
> whites in Central High School tomorrow, the
> evidence of discord, anger, and resentment
> has come to me from so many sources as
> to become a deluge. There is evidence of
> disorder and threats of disorder which
> could have but one inevitable result—that
> is, violence which can lead to injury and the
> doing of harm to persons and property.

I could hardly believe my ears. Were white men and women in Little Rock really so angry about black students attending Central that they were willing to harm us? The thought that people were threatening violence at first made me more angry than afraid. But I found an odd sense of comfort in what Governor Faubus said next:

> Units of the National Guard have been or are
> now being mobilized . . . Advance units are
> already on duty on the grounds of Central
> High School . . . [to] maintain . . . the peace
> and order of the community . . .

It was shocking to think that a military unit might be necessary to keep the peace on my first day at Central, but I still wanted to go. I honestly believed that I was included in those whom our governor had deployed the Arkansas National Guard to protect. Somehow, I had gotten it into my head that Central was crucial to my future. I knew that if I could make it there—a school ranked among the top forty in the nation—I could make it anywhere. Things would settle down eventually, I figured. In the meantime, the National Guard would keep me safe—or so I thought. When I closed my eyes that night, I was confident that I would be at Central the next day and that I would be safe.

It would be my last night of innocence.

The next morning, I woke up to news that the opening of school was delayed. Mrs. Bates, the pretty black NAACP organizer I had met outside Central on the day I went to register for classes, had called my parents. She reported that the school board was asking the black students to stay at home until further notice. Between the National Guard's disruptive presence and Governor Faubus's call for a delay in desegregating Central, the school board had made a decision: They wanted to seek further legal resolution and take the issue of desegregating to a judge.

What does that mean? I wondered. I'd pinned so much of my hope and excitement on this day. Now, all I could do was wait and wonder. It was beyond frustrating. One thing was clear, that my new outfit would have to wait.

The day seemed to drag with little information from the adults involved. Daddy went to work, as usual, and Mother spent much of the time on the telephone, answering questions from concerned relatives and friends. She also checked in with Mrs. Bates for updates. Most of my own friends had returned to Mann that day, so I couldn't even talk to them on the telephone.

By early afternoon, U.S. District Court judge Ronald Davies ordered the school system to proceed the next day with integration at Central. He said he was not swayed by the sentiments of the segregationists.

"I have a constitutional duty and obligation from which I shall not shrink," he said.

Later that afternoon, Superintendent Blossom called a last-minute meeting with our parents and instructed them to send us to Central the next day alone. Their own presence might spur even more trouble at the school, he told them. My parents could have decided right then that the risks were too high and withdrawn me from Central. I'm grateful that they did not. Instead, they remained calm and resolute. In a rare newspaper interview, Daddy later explained to an *Arkansas Gazette* reporter why he didn't back down:

"Only one thought ever crossed my mind about the whole thing. She had a right to go there. My tax money is not separated from the rest of the tax money. There was no reason for her to pass one high school to go to another."

Besides Ernie and Gloria, I wasn't sure who else would join me at Central. Several black students had changed their minds when they heard that they would have to give up their extracurricular activities. I'd just have to wait and see.

Sometime after midnight, Mrs. Bates called again to tell my parents to drop me off at eight thirty a.m. about a block from the school. An interracial group of ministers would meet us there to escort us inside, she said. We wouldn't have to walk alone.

The next morning, September 4, I popped out of bed, full of anticipation. It was really going to happen, I thought. Questions filled my head: Who else would be there from Dunbar and Mann? What would the teachers be like? What about the students? Would I make new friends? Was I ready to compete with them academically? How long would it take me to learn my way around that huge campus?

As Mother and I drove over, we noticed a small group of students and two black ministers gathering near the intersection. This was the meeting spot, and Mother pulled to a stop. She looked relieved when she saw Reverend Harry Bass, who had been my pastor at White Memorial. Mother also knew the other black minister who was there, Reverend Z. Z. Dryver, the father of one of my friends at Dunbar. She trusted these men, and I'm sure it comforted her to leave me in such good hands. Three older white ministers and a young white man, none of whom I knew, were there, too.

I said goodbye to Mother, hopped out of the car, and made my way over to the group. As I walked toward them, I saw Ernie, Gloria, and another student I recognized, Jefferson Thomas, a fellow sophomore who had been president of the student council at Dunbar the previous year. I had worked closely with him as vice president, so I knew him pretty well. There were three students I didn't know, but I learned their names quickly: Thelma Mothershed, Minnijean Brown, and Jane Hill, a tall, quiet girl who seemed a bit more uncomfortable than the rest. We chatted anxiously until one of the ministers approached and said it was time to get moving. But first, he said, we needed to pray. We formed a tight circle and bowed our heads as the reverend asked God to walk with us, strengthen and protect us. Then the adults put us in formation. Out front were the four white men: Reverend Dunbar Ogden, Jr., and his twenty-one-year-old son, David; Reverend Will Campbell; and Reverend George Chauncey. The students lined up by twos in the middle. Reverends Bass and Dryver held up the rear.

It was time to go.

Slowly and silently, our group began moving up the street toward the school. I could hear the rumble of a crowd up ahead. It was loud, like a football game crowd. I clutched my notebook and moved with the group through the sticky September air. With every step, the hooting and hollering grew louder. As we got closer to Fourteenth Street, I glanced toward the Mobil gas station on the other side of the street, and for the first time I saw it—a mob of people that stretched as far as I could see.

The sheer size of the crowd was shocking. There must have been hundreds of people—white mothers with faces contorted in anger, white fathers pumping their fists in the air and shouting, white teenagers and children waving Confederate flags and mimicking their parents. Just who were these people? Were they the women who turned up their noses and murmured nasty words at Mother and me on the city bus? Were they the white customers I saw from time to time with Big Daddy at the meatpacking houses downtown? Were they my white neighbors? The scene felt surreal. With everyone screaming and jeering at once, their words sounded muddled, except one: *nigger . . . nigger . . . nigger.* It shot out of angry mouths like bullets and pierced my ears again and again.

Adrenaline pulsed through my body and quickened the pace of my heart. I had never seen such raw anger up close before. And this was directed at me. For what? Because I wanted to go to school? I turned away and re-membered Mother's and Daddy's words:

*They're just ignorant, low-class people. They're just try-ing to scare you. Do not stoop to their level. You are a Walls. Just take the next step, and the next.*

The mob was too far away to stop me from getting in-side. The front entrance of the school was now in sight, and the military was just steps ahead.

Finally, we were staring into the faces of the Arkan-sas National Guard. The guardsmen had formed a ring around the school. They blocked the entrance, but I was certain that when they saw us, they would step aside and allow us through. They were, after all, there to protect us and keep out the troublemakers, I thought. But not one of them budged. Instead, the commander, Lieutenant Colo-nel Marion Johnson, stepped forward. I noticed that he had both hands clutched unnaturally tight around a billy club. His knuckles looked white. Ernie, pressing his lips together nervously, stood beside me. Gloria stood behind me, and behind her, Jane towered over us all. Johnson told Reverend Ogden that on the orders of Faubus, we would not be permitted to enter the school.

The commander's words stunned me. There was a huge disconnect in my head. The guardsmen weren't there to protect us; they were there to keep us out. As the message washed over me, I thought:

*You've got to be kidding.*

Ernie, the only senior among us, spoke up: "You're not going to let us in? Is that what you're telling us?"

The officer repeated his order for us to leave. His men stayed in formation, still blocking us out, their rifles slung across their chests. Our group stood there for a moment, not quite sure what to do. And then the ministers turned and led us silently away. The mob continued yelling in the distance, but this time, I barely heard any of it. I was completely stunned. The highest court in the land had said I had a right to be at that school just like the white children. What would it take to open those closed ears and change their hardened hearts?

For the rest of the day, I felt out of sync, isolated. I kept thinking that all my good friends were in school, where I should have been. But as bad as I felt, nothing could compare with the sorrow that came over me when I clicked on the television news that evening and saw in black and white what had happened to Elizabeth Eckford, a junior who was supposed to be with our group that day.

I didn't know Elizabeth personally, but our families knew each other. Her grandfather owned a neighborhood grocery store just across the street from Big Daddy's pool hall and café. But the Eckfords didn't have a telephone, so Elizabeth didn't get the word about our meeting place that morning. Unfortunately, Elizabeth walked right into the mob, alone, which surrounded and terrorized her. There she was on my television screen, walking silently in her crisp black-and-white dress. Her face looked solemn, and she wore dark sunglasses, which I'm sure must have hidden tears. She was followed by some of the same angry men, women, and children I had seen from a distance earlier that day. But they were right on Elizabeth, shouting at her, spitting at her, clawing at her, not the least bit concerned that television cameras were capturing it all for eternity. That iconic image of Elizabeth surrounded by the mob would circle the globe and outrage the world.

The next day, the *New York Times* would run this account of the moment when a lone white woman—Grace Lorch, whose husband taught at Philander Smith College—came to Elizabeth's aid:

> The Negro girl . . . sat on a bench. She seemed
> in a state of shock. A white woman, Mrs. Grace
> Lorch, walked over to comfort her.
>
> "What are you doing, you nigger lover?"

Mrs. Lorch was asked. "You stay away from that girl."

"She's scared," Mrs. Lorch said. "She's just a little girl." She appealed to the men and women around her.

"Why don't you calm down?" she asked. "I'm not here to fight with you. Six months from now you'll be ashamed of what you're doing."

"Go home, you're just one of them," Mrs. Lorch was told.

She escorted the Negro student to the other side of the street, but the crowd followed.

"Won't somebody please call a taxi?" she pleaded. She was met with hoot calls and jeers.

Finally, after being jostled by the crowd, she worked her way to the street corner, and the two boarded a bus.

Two others who were supposed to be part of our group, Melba Pattillo and Terrence Roberts, both juniors, also walked separately into the mob that morning. But each of them managed to slip away. I didn't know Melba, but Terrence had been president of the student council at Dunbar while I was vice president in my eighth-grade year. That would have been ten black students who showed up with intentions to enter Central. But after that morning, Jane Hill, the tall, quiet girl who had made that first terrible walk with us, never returned.

That left nine of us.

None of us had any idea how long it would be before we were allowed to go to school. One day turned into two days, which turned into a week and then another. During that time, when I wasn't at home, the nine of us were at Mr. and Mrs. Bates's house. The couple lived on West Twenty-Eighth Street in a middle-class neighborhood with small wood-and-brick houses. The house on West Twenty-Eighth Street became the unofficial headquarters for the nine of us trying to enter Central. We were interviewed by journalists there, we met politicians there, and we heard words of encouragement and lectures about the importance of our mission there. It became our home away from home, and Mr. and Mrs. Bates were our trusted guardians.

Mr. Bates was tall and lean, with a narrow face, deep brown skin, and short gray hair. He was grandfatherly to me, very low-key, gentle, and reassuring. While he was a longtime activist who used his newspaper to advocate for civil rights, it was Mrs. Bates who rose to the limelight. She wouldn't be caught anywhere without being perfectly made up, head to toe, but pity the man who mistook her ladylike ways as a sign of weakness. She was tough, with razor-sharp edges. And she demanded respect.

Over the weeks that my cohorts and I were banned from school, Mrs. Bates became our point person—the one who arranged media interviews and often the one who spoke for us. She was naturally at ease under the glow of television lights and quick to fire off the perfect quote. But I was uncomfortable with the constant throng of people always around us, asking questions, taking pictures. No matter the time of day or night, it seemed somebody was always at the Bateses' house. Journalists. Politicians. NAACP fieldworkers.

When I could, I'd slip away from them all, find a quiet corner somewhere, pull out my books, and at least try to look busy—a tactic I began using to deflect attention. When the nine of us were together as a group, I tried to just fade into the background. I never liked the feeling of being on display. I think Mrs. Bates eventually came to understand that about me and just let me be. I always appreciated that about her. She took a lot of the heat off our parents, too. They weren't hounded by the press and got to stay mostly in the background. For that leadership, she was already paying a heavy price—threatening telephone calls every day, a cross burned in her yard, and a rock slammed through her window in the middle of the night, with a message that promised dynamite the next time. And the nine of us hadn't even made it inside the school yet.

After the first week of our missing classes, Mrs. Bates arranged for teachers at Central to send homework packets so we could at least make a valiant effort to keep up with our classmates. I saw my schedule for the first time when I received a homework packet. I was enrolled in English, geometry, biology, Spanish, gym, and speech. A group of Philander Smith professors and other teachers tutored us and help with our schoolwork. Dr. Lorch—an anti-racist activist and husband of Grace Lorch, who had helped Elizabeth on her first harrowing day at Central— was particularly helpful to me with my geometry homework. I occasionally took the bus to Philander Smith in the afternoon or evening when he was available to work with me. When I finished my schoolwork, I turned it in to Mrs. Bates, who arranged to get it to our teachers.

But I missed going to school. I missed chatting with peers and making new friends. I missed the daily interaction with teachers, the give-and-take in the classroom that sometimes helped the textbooks make sense. I wondered how long it would be before I got to meet them all face-to-face. Would they resent my presence as much as the mob that still gathered each morning outside the school? I grew more and more anxious that I was falling behind, especially since no one seemed to have any idea how long the wait would be. I think all nine of us felt that way.

Clusters of us had known one another before our fates thrust us together, but during all those meetings and meals at the home of Mr. and Mrs. Bates, the nine of us began getting to know one another as friends. On television, we often heard ourselves referred to as "the nine" or "the Little Rock Nine" in the same way that people sometimes identify twins, as if they have no separate identities. But we were growing more comfortable around one another, and I was starting to get a real sense of the distinct personalities. Ernie was the oldest, cool-headed and serious. His status as the lone senior seemed to catapult him into the position of our leader. He was usually the one Mrs. Bates and the press grabbed to speak for the group. Melba and Minnijean were the outgoing ones. They were also good friends, singers, and quite comfortable in front of the cameras. Terry was a young intellectual who was always at the top of his class. But he also had a fun side, a dry, witty sense of humor that kept me in stitches. Elizabeth seemed painfully shy. She had expressive doe eyes that seemed to reveal a hint of sadness. She could barely even make eye contact when she spoke. There was a sweet innocence about her and an easy, trusting nature. Thelma was quiet, too, but she seemed the most fragile among us. Aside from being physically small, she had a heart condition that made everybody want to protect her. Jefferson was a sopho-more, like me, and everyone's pampered baby brother, a bit naive, but athletic and smart. He was always joking around and somehow seemed to find humor in even the most serious situations. He also loved music and had an unbelievably large and varied record collection. Gloria was the other sophomore. She was mature and dignified, petite and dainty. She also had what most teenagers en-vied: her own car.

I had a December birthday, which made me the youngest of the bunch, but from the time I was a little girl, people always said that something about me seemed old. Maybe it's my way with all kinds of people. I don't know. But I got along well with everybody, and in the days ahead, I would be called in to referee when some of the personalities began to collide.

Mrs. Bates understood our anxiety, and tried her best to assure us that things would be resolved soon. The law-yer Thurgood Marshall was coming to town to represent us, she said. That really excited me. He was already high on my list of heroes. Even before successfully presenting the *Brown* case in the Supreme Court, he had argued a case in Little Rock that involved my uncle Byron Johnson. He was among a group of black teachers at Dunbar who had demanded equal pay with the white teachers in the 1940s. The NAACP and Marshall took on the Little Rock

School Board in that case and won. I knew we were in good hands.

The local newspapers and the black press helped me keep up with the confusing zigzag of events that followed: Just three days after the National Guard blocked our entry into Central, the school board was back in court, asking for its own desegregation plan to be suspended. Judge Davies refused the request.

Then the U.S. Justice Department asked the court to force the governor to comply with the desegregation order. The department's investigation had found no truth to the governor's claims that he called out the National Guard to "keep the peace" based on evidence that violence would erupt at Central if black students were admitted. The investigation determined that Governor Faubus had, in fact, clearly acted purely as a segregationist with the sole purpose of keeping out the black students. Judge Davies scheduled the courtroom showdown on that matter for September 20.

I had never been inside a courtroom until that day. My friend Bunny, who was home from the private school she attended in North Carolina, went along to offer her support. I didn't know what to expect, and as we walked inside, I could feel my palms getting sweaty. The courtroom was still, dark, and quiet. I could almost hear myself breathe. I took a seat near the front. When the judge entered, he sat behind the large mahogany desk before us. He was small and serious. But my eyes stayed mostly on Mr. Marshall. Bunny and I were mesmerized by this attorney who had the swagger and aura of a movie star. I had never seen a black professional with more confidence. Here was a black man striding up and down this courtroom with the certainty that this was where he belonged. Tall and lean, with closely cropped black hair, he was as handsome as he was smart. And he did not tread lightly. I suppose I had been conditioned to expect quiet deference from a black lawyer practicing in a room full of white people. But not this man. He spoke his mind, and he did so unapologetically, indignantly. He commanded respect, and respect is what he got, especially from Judge Davies.

I added Judge Davies to my list of civil rights heroes that day, too. He treated Mr. Marshall with the respect he deserved, a respect that might not have been as forthcoming if one of the other white southern judges had been presiding.

In stature, Judge Davies stood barely five feet tall. But he was fearless in the face of segregationists willing to try just about anything to have their way. Like Marshall, the judge didn't mince words.

Governor Faubus didn't attend the September 20 hearing. Instead, he sent his attorneys. But they soon grew frustrated after Judge Davies overruled them several times. Before the hearing was over, they gathered their papers and announced that they were leaving. It caused quite a buzz in the courtroom. Judge Davies slapped his gavel on the desk.

"The hearing will continue," he boomed.

I was so proud of Ernie and Elizabeth, who were called to testify. They answered questions thoughtfully and articulately about why they wanted to attend Central and what happened when we had tried to enter on September 4. And of course, Mr. Marshall did not disappoint. He gave a rousing closing argument. In one simple but powerful moment, he turned and pointed at Ernie, Minnie, and me, shook his head, full of righteous indignation, and said:

"These young people should be in school."

Judge Davies didn't take long to render his decision: The National Guard had to go. Faubus could no longer use the troops to block our entrance into Central. With that, Davies banged his gavel once more, and court was adjourned.

I was absolutely jubilant. I'd just seen everything I'd learned about the Constitution, the judicial process, and justice come to life. Justice had been served. I assumed that meant our ordeal was finally over. I turned to Mrs. Bates and said:

"This means we can go to school!"

Her caution caught me off guard.

"We'll see," she responded, not sounding excited at all.

I was disappointed. I didn't understand her lack of enthusiasm.

That night, Governor Faubus went on the radio to make an announcement. He would withdraw the troops from Central, he said, as the federal order had demanded. But he lambasted Judge Davies and the Department of Justice. He urged the NAACP to back off its integration plans. And he threatened the possibility of bloodshed—yet did nothing to discourage the violence.

I went to bed that night feeling completely deflated. Anything could happen. Bunny was headed back to school in North Carolina. The National Guard was gone. And the governor was peddling fear. After what I'd seen of that mob outside Central, I couldn't be sure that his threat wasn't real.

Outdoors, a storm raged, casting a gloomy pall over the entire city. The weather was mimicking my mood. The big day was set for Monday, September 23. But a world of doubt lay between this moment and that one. Mrs. Bates was right. I'd just have to wait and see.

# CHAPTER 5

## D-Day

When I opened my eyes the morning of September 23, the first thing I noticed was the beaming sun. After such a wet and gloomy weekend, this was surely a good sign. Once again, I put on my new outfit.

The plan was to meet at the home of Mr. and Mrs. Bates. There, we would get instructions from the city police, which now had the responsibility of protecting us. When Mother and I arrived, the front yard and living room were abuzz with media snapping photographs, shooting television footage, conducting interviews, and darting here and there. As usual, I skirted past them and joined the other students. We chatted anxiously about our "first" day of school—which classes we had, which ones we feared, what our teachers might be like. I think all of us recognized what *could* happen. We'd seen the mob outside the school. Elizabeth had even been close enough to feel its wrath. But I didn't want to talk—or even think—about the danger. None of us did.

The police instructed us to be transported to a side entrance of the school, away from the crowd out front. It was time for us to go, Mrs. Bates said. We hugged our parents and headed out. Before going out the door, I glanced back at Mother, and she had that look on her face again—the smile that didn't match the worry in her eyes. The nine of us then piled into two cars, driven by NAACP officials, for the short ride to Central.

As we drew closer to the side of the school, I could hear the muffled sounds of a crowd beyond the car's closed windows. I knew the mob was back. They were not going to give up their fight easily. But neither was I. The cars carrying us rolled up to the curb, next to the side entrance. The drivers hopped out and yanked open the car doors. Suddenly, the chants and jeers of the crowd sounded deafening:

"Two, four, six, eight, we ain't gonna integrate . . ."

I stepped out of the car and moved swiftly behind the other students toward the side of the building. I had no time to think or worry about what the crowd was saying or doing. Just take one step and then another, I told my-self. In no time, all nine of us were rushed through a set of large double doors, which closed quickly behind us and shut out the light. No one made a sound, but we kept moving through the darkness. I just followed the footsteps up some stairs and then up another set, into the light. Next, there was a long hallway. Finally, we stopped just outside the main office, where we were met by a primly dressed white woman with glasses and graying hair. She seemed very professional and pleasant enough as she handed us our schedules and pointed the way to our classes. I would come to know her as Elizabeth Huckaby, my English teacher and the vice principal for girls.

While my eight comrades and I were heading to our classes for the first time, the crowd outside was growing steadily and working itself into a frenzy. The chaos had started even before we arrived. News photographers and reporters captured the upheaval that unfurled when four black journalists who had been with us at the Bateses' home made it to the scene just moments ahead of us.

Alex Wilson, editor of the Memphis-based *Tri-State Defender,* and Moses Newson, on assignment for the *Baltimore Afro-American,* led the way, inching toward the rowdy crowd to cover the scene. They were followed by James L. Hicks, editor of the *Amsterdam News* in New York, and Earl Davy, a photographer who often took photos for the newspaper owned by Mr. and Mrs. Bates. Two white men began following them.

"Go home, you son of a bitch nigger!" one of them yelled.

A few more white men leapt in front of the journalists with outstretched hands to block their path.

"We are newspapermen," Wilson retorted.

"We only want to do our jobs," Hicks added.

But the taunting continued. The crowd quickly swelled, and mayhem broke out. Someone threatened a lynching. Others lunged into the black journalists, kicking, punching, and spitting at them. The attackers slammed Davy's Graflex camera to the concrete sidewalk and chased him, while another group attacked Newson and Hicks until they were finally able to escape. Wilson, a former war correspondent, had seen this kind of hatred up close as he traveled throughout the South covering civil rights, including the Emmett Till trial in the fall of 1955. As Wilson picked up his wide-brimmed hat and straightened himself, one of the ringleaders ordered him to run. But Wilson, a lanky ex-Marine who stood six feet four inches tall, refused. Incensed by this man's proud composure, the mob grew more virulent in their attack. Finally, one of them delivered a crushing blow to the back of Wilson's head with a heavy object believed to have been a brick. The tall black man tumbled to the ground. In his own account of the incident, Wilson later wrote that a vision of Elizabeth Eckford "as she with dignity strode through a jeering, hooting gauntlet of segregationists" had flashed in his mind and given him the courage to face the mob on his feet. But Wilson never fully recovered from the beating. He developed a nervous condition widely reported as Parkinson's disease and died three years later at age fifty-one.

I was horrified when I saw the attack on the evening news. These black reporters were risking their own lives to tell our collective story. They were accomplished professionals, but in the Klan territory throughout Mississippi, Alabama, and on this day Little Rock, they were reviled. But they kept coming and kept writing, long before the mainstream press jumped on board.

Eventually that morning, someone in the crowd recognized that while the journalists were being savagely beaten, the nine of us were entering the school building. The hysteria immediately shifted our way. By then, though, the doors already had shut behind us. Benjamin Fine, the *New York Times* reporter who had catapulted our story to the front page of his newspaper weeks earlier, gave this account:

> "They've gone in," a man shouted.
> "Oh, God," said a woman, "the niggers are in school."
> A group of six girls, dressed in skirts and sweaters, hair in ponytails, started to shriek and wail.

"The niggers are in our school," they howled hysterically.

One of them jumped up and down on the sidewalk, waving her arms toward her classmates in the school who were looking out of the windows, and screamed over and over again:

"Come on out, come on out."

Tears flowed down her face, her body shook in uncontrollable spasms.

Three of her classmates grew hysterical, and threw their arms around each other. They began dancing up and down.

"The niggers are in," they shrieked, "come on out of the school. Don't stay there with the niggers. Come on out . . . come on . . ."

As that sickening spate of violence unfolded, I was likely stepping into my first class of the day, Mrs. Huckaby's English class, where I was oblivious to the commotion outside. As soon as I walked into her classroom, she directed me to a desk in the first row, two seats from the door. She wasn't particularly warm, but I would come to understand that it had nothing to do with me; she treated everyone the same. But I could tell from the outset that she was fair. She didn't tolerate any name-calling, and at the first sight of any bullying, she shut it down immediately. She wouldn't hesitate to file a disciplinary report, she warned, and since she was an administrator, her threat carried weight.

As I slid into my chair in her class that morning, I could feel all eyes fastened on me. That was one of the things I hated most—being the center of attention. My insides knotted with dread. I wished to be invisible. I stared at my desktop, the hardwood floors, Mrs. Huckaby's face, anywhere to avoid the hot gaze of my classmates. Mrs. Huckaby didn't miss a beat, trying to go on with class as though this were a regular day. But there was nothing regular about it. I tried mightily, but I couldn't concentrate. Why wouldn't they stop staring at me?

Finally, the bell rang, but momentary relief turned quickly to even more serious dread. Hundreds of students spilled from their classes into the halls. The noise level was louder than the loudest football game I'd ever attended. Every face in the crowd was white, and they all seemed to be staring at me, sneering at me. A group of slick-haired boys in black leather jackets and white T-shirts—poor imitations of James Dean—purposely walked too close, bumped me hard with their shoulders, and swaggered off, laughing at "that nigger." The word was slung at me so often that day that my heart turned almost numb. I tried to tune out their words, their stares, and their finger-pointing, but it was impossible.

A few students looked my way sympathetically,

almost as though they were ashamed of their school-mates' behavior. But they also seemed afraid to smile, afraid to say hello, afraid to be seen showing even minimal empathy. Their sympathetic eyes quickly looked away as soon as they met mine.

I yearned to see a kind face, something or someone familiar. Where were the other black students? I saw no sign of them anywhere. I felt so completely alone. Somehow, I made it to my second- and third-period classes and each time was assigned to the first row, a couple of seats from the door.

By third period, my nerves were starting to settle a bit. This was geometry, the class I most feared. My teacher, Margaret Reiman, was a strict disciplinarian who, like Mrs. Huckaby, didn't tolerate any nonsense. She would put up with no disruptions, she announced firmly. We had much work to do, and she moved quickly into the business of class. The atmosphere was calm for about the first twenty minutes. Then came a knock on the door. I was close enough to see a uniformed officer standing on the other side. Mrs. Reiman walked to the door and stuck her head out. I kept my eyes on the two of them as they talked briefly. As my teacher stepped back into the class, I searched her face for clues. Was something wrong? But her face was blank as she announced:

"Carlotta Walls, get your books and follow the gentleman outside."

Get my books? My heart sank. I knew I was leaving again for the day.

"Follow me," the officer said, turning quickly and stepping speedily down the hall.

This time, the hallway was empty and quiet, except for the officer's heavy footsteps. As I tried to keep pace with him, my mind turned back to geometry. I couldn't afford to miss another math class. This was my weakest subject. I didn't know anyone yet, so how would I be able to make up the next day's assignment? I'd missed far too much already. Once I stepped inside the office, though, all thoughts about geometry stopped. I could tell right away that something was seriously wrong. My eight comrades were already gathered there with their books. They looked frightened and confused. Before I could ask any questions, another officer commanded: "This way!"

I almost had to trot to keep up. I had no idea where we were going or why, but we were in a hurry. It was like being led through a maze. Finally, we arrived in the mechanics classroom, an enclosed garage on the ground level. Two police cars sat parked inside the garage. An officer instructed us to get in quickly.

"Lie low and hide," he told us, handing us several blankets.

Then, to the driver: "Put your foot to the floor. And don't stop for anything."

Now I was terrified. We were on the run from something, but what? As I lay crouched on the back seat, I lifted my head from under the blanket. I had to see what was going on. If I was going to die, I wanted to see it coming.

The two police cars shot out of the garage into the light and sped down a gravel drive, past the Campus Inn, the diner where the white students hung out for burgers and Cokes at lunch. As we whizzed down Sixteenth Street, past the stadium, away from the school, I craned my neck but couldn't see anything more than the back of the school. The four of us were too frightened even to speak. The officer sped down streets and whipped around corners until he had dropped the other students off at their homes. I was the last one to be dropped off. By the time he pulled to a stop in front of my house, my heart was sprinting.

Mother met me at the door. This time, she didn't even try to hide her fear. Her eyes were red. I'm certain that her jet-black hair started graying that day. She threw her arms around me.

"Are you okay?" she asked repeatedly.

News of the mob had been on the radio all morning, she said. Newscasters were saying the crowd had grown to more than one thousand people and that police could no longer control them. That's when I realized why we had left in such a hurry. Relatives had been calling all day, and their message was unified: Get Carlotta out of that school!

I retreated to my room and took off my new outfit. Maybe, I thought, the darn thing brought bad luck. I slipped on my "after-school" clothes, plopped down on the living room sofa, and stared out the window in front of the house. My eyes fell on my church up the road. I wondered: Where was God in all of this? Was it He who had spared us from the wrath of that mob? What if they had gotten inside? Would they really have lynched us?

I couldn't understand their fury. All this because they didn't want their children to sit next to me in school? I had heard white parents complain in television interviews that school integration could lead to race mixing and interracial marriage. Was this the source of their rage? If so, it seemed nuts to me. Would my first day at Central be my last? There was nothing left to do but wait.

At this time, Little Rock mayor Woodrow Mann sent a telegram to President Dwight D. Eisenhower. The city and state police had tried to control the mob at Central, Mayor Mann wrote, but the situation ultimately was considered too unsafe for the nine of us to remain in school.

News reports painted a picture of a city out of control, with random mobs roaming the streets, terrorizing any black residents they could find. In black neighborhoods throughout the city, lights were off, curtains were drawn, and streets were still and quiet.

The same day, President Eisenhower released a statement:

"I want to make several things very clear in connection with the disgraceful occurrences of today at Central High School in the city of Little Rock," he began.

"The federal law and orders of a United States District Court, implementing that law, cannot be flouted with impunity by any individual, or any mob of extremists . . . ," he continued. "It will be a sad day for this country—both at home and abroad—if school children can safely attend their classes only under the protection of armed guards."

President Eisenhower also issued an emergency proclamation barring anyone from blocking the school and interfering with the federal court's desegregation order—meaning the order not from local or state government but from the whole United States government. But the next morning, I awakened to news reports that the mob had again gathered outside Central—one thousand people strong.

I spent the day indoors, glued to the television. The telephone rang constantly. Mother and Daddy would dash to make it to the phone before my sisters or me. Sometimes, they just stood there quietly for a few seconds and hung up without saying a word. But sometimes, I could see the anger on Daddy's face as he slammed down the receiver. Neither of them ever said a word to me about those phone calls, but they didn't have to. I knew what was going on. I knew it was those nasty men and women from the street, and I could only imagine the vile words they spat into the phone. I hated to see the worry I was causing Mother and Daddy. This was a particularly low day for me. When would it all end? Would we ever get inside and get to meet our classmates at Central without the circus atmosphere? Would they ever stop being so small-minded and fearful and just get to know us?

Finally, President Eisenhower followed up on his promise that his actions would be "quick, hard, and decisive" and signed an executive order to use military force to protect the nine of us. That night, I watched with my family as the president announced on television that he had called out the troops of the 101st Airborne Division to ensure we'd be escorted inside safely.

My spirits perked up. Over one thousand paratroopers were already on their way to Little Rock, President Eisenhower said. He also announced that he was placing the Arkansas National Guard under federal orders. This was a historic move, the first time a U.S. president had called on the military to enforce a federal school desegregation order.

My first thought was: What took so long? I still wish it had happened sooner, but I am tremendously grateful that President Eisenhower stepped in when he did. Finally, I would be able to return to school—and with the protection of the U.S. military, no less.

Later that night, Uncle J.W., a World War II veteran, called to tell me about the 101st Airborne. They were America's military elite, renowned for their heroism during World War II. Now they were coming to Little Rock. Now I surely would be in good hands, he said.

For the first night in a long time, I slept peacefully.

I woke up extra early on September 25. A mix of nervous anticipation and excitement jolted me out of bed before sunrise, even though I wasn't sure I would be allowed to go to school. Sometime before daybreak, though, Mrs. Bates showed up at our door with instructions. We were to meet at her house by eight a.m., she told my parents. Superintendent Blossom had called her after midnight to say that the military troopers would meet the nine of us at her house later that morning and escort us to school. To make sure we all got the message, Mrs. Bates drove to each of our homes.

Yes, I was going to school, mother said when I was up, revealing—as usual—just what I needed to know, nothing more. I got dressed quickly and grabbed a bite to eat. I couldn't wait to see what this elite military unit looked like. Mother and I pulled up outside the home of Mr. and Mrs. Bates as the other students and their parents were getting out of their cars, too. The place was already swarming with reporters, photographers, neighbors, and NAACP officials. We went into the Bateses' home, making small talk until everyone arrived.

The atmosphere was noticeably lighter. One of the ministers in the room led us all in prayer. Heads were bowed, and tears rolled down many cheeks as the minister asked God to protect and guide us on this historic day.

Suddenly, a loud rumble startled everyone. Military jeeps were making their way down the quiet street. The army was here! A wave of excitement rushed through the room. We dashed to the living room window to get a closer look. Soldiers dressed in helmets and combat gear hopped out and stood at attention with their rifles. Mrs. Bates called us away from the windows. It was time, she said. We gathered our books and made our way to the door. I felt more ready than I'd ever been for this moment. As we stepped outside, cameras flashed around us from high and low. Reporters shouted questions and jotted in small notebooks. Black mothers and fathers, who had been held captive inside their homes for days by the rampaging white mob, spilled onto front porches, yards, and the sides of streets.

One by one, the nine of us climbed into a station wagon. A topless jeep filled with soldiers led the way. Another followed us. This time, we drove at a normal pace. This time, there was no speeding or trying to hide from the mob. The U.S. military had tucked all nine of us securely under its wing, and in just a few minutes, we would fly right into the heart of Central, almost daring those hateful men and women to try to put their hands on us now.

The streets were as quiet as a graveyard, except for the occasional crackle of the soldiers' walkie-talkies. Soldiers lined the streets of the school, snapping to attention when our station wagon pulled up. This time, we passed by the side door we had entered on that terrifying first day. Instead, our caravan pulled to a stop right in front of the school. This time, I—we—had a right to walk through those front doors, like anyone else. And the president of the United States had sent our U.S. military to ensure that right.

The car doors swung open. It was 9:22 a.m. My heart thumped faster than ever before. As I stepped out of the station wagon, the morning sky seemed brighter. Twenty-two soldiers surrounded us, all of us striding ahead up the stairs to school. I felt safe, protected, and proud.

Finally, I stood at that grand entrance with its heavy wooden doors. I took a deep breath. The granite eyes of those four Greek gods and goddesses above my head seemed to peer down at me: Ambition. Personality. Opportunity. Preparation. Walk with me now, I implored.

And with a new sense of calm, I stepped across the threshold.

# CHAPTER 6

## The Blessing of Walls

To my surprise, getting inside Central was just the beginning of a brand-new struggle: finding a way to survive. I wanted to believe that the cold stares, the name-calling and taunts I had experienced on the first day would soon melt away. That the mobs would disappear for good now that the U.S. military's best stood guard. That the racist troublemakers would turn their attention elsewhere. That eventually Central would embrace me.

It wouldn't take long for those hopes to fade.

Ernie and Melba have said that, for them, each day was a war. For me, it was more an internal battle: How do I dodge the wannabe James Deans? How do I hold my books to avoid attack? How do I manage to get through the day without using my locker or going to the girls' bathroom? Calculating my every move was consuming—and draining.

There was no training for us in self-defense or in the ways of protest. That came years later for the college students who sparked the sit-in movement at lunch counters throughout the South. Our "training" was on the job. And my earliest lessons came in the hallways between classes.

The noise in the halls of Central was earsplitting the first month. Just imagine a constant stream of about two thousand raucous teenagers heading in all different directions over five floors. Add to the mix the prejudice against the nine new black students, and the atmosphere was volatile—even with the presence of our military guards. Each of us had been assigned a military escort to accompany us through the day. The troopers usually waited outside the classroom door until it was time to move to the next class. But while the soldiers were there to make sure the nine of us stayed alive, for anything short of that, I was pretty much on my own. A lot just seemed to escape their ears and eyes, and I'm not sure if it was intentional or not.

Like the spitting, for instance.

The band of boys in the black leather jackets were the worst offenders. They seemed to have come from the woods with their dank, moldy smell and their facial stubble, and they made a sport of spitting on me. If you've ever been hit by a nasty gob, you know how disgusting it is, how humiliating, how infuriating. The first time, the wet slime came flying out of nowhere, landing on the bottom left side of my face. I was trying to work my way through the crowded halls between classes on my second day inside when, without warning, I felt something wet hit my face. I flinched. Immediately, I knew what it was. But who had done it? It was useless trying to single out the villain in the sea of smirking faces quickly moving past me. Was it one of the black-leather boys? Or did it come from one of their ponytailed girlfriends? In either case, there was nothing I could do to respond.

I had already been warned against retaliation by Dr. Blossom before school even started; responding in kind could lead to my expulsion. And tears were out of the question. I couldn't let them see my hurt. I couldn't give them that kind of power. So, without a word, I wiped my face against the sleeve of my dress and kept on trekking. From then on, I stayed on guard, scanning eyes and mouths as I traveled the halls. I learned to jump back quickly or duck to avoid being hit in the face. But I always carried Kleenex, just in case.

When the black-leather boys or their girl sidekicks walked close to me and knocked my books out of my hand, I learned never to bend over right away to pick them up, lest I provide the perfect target to get kicked in the backside and onto my face.

The first time it happened, I was completely blind-sided. I usually carried my books because I didn't like leaving anything in my locker. It was frequently the target of vandals, as were the lockers of the other eight. The vandals often left crude handwritten notes, like "Nigger go back to Africa." They sometimes took our books and destroyed our homework. So I usually piled into my arms as much as I could carry. After my books went sailing across the floor, I leaned over to pick them up, and somebody else whacked me with a foot in the bottom. I heard laughter in the background as I went down flat on my face. Stunned and embarrassed, I hopped quickly back onto my feet.

The harassers were fast and sneaky, and they didn't seem at all threatened by the military presence. When I pointed out the assailants, the guard could only direct them to the office.

The entire situation made me angry. I was angry that I had to face this kind of torture in a hallowed place of learning, angry that the threat to my life was so great that I needed to be escorted to class by battle-trained soldiers, yet those same soldiers didn't even have the authority to stop groups of hateful boys and girls from spitting on me and knocking me on my face.

Well, I'd always heard that what doesn't kill you just makes you stronger. If I learned nothing else that year, I learned that. I did grow mentally tougher. I resolved that if the soldiers couldn't protect me, I'd have to do it myself. As I saw it, part of my job was to avoid making the same mistake twice. That one tumble onto my face taught me to carry my books on the side closer to the wall and never next to the open hallway. And when I had to bend over, I learned to turn my backside to the wall as well. Thank goodness for the walls. At times, they seemed the only protectors I had.

The bullies always traveled in groups, and with all the noise and distractions in the halls, their antics could easily escape notice. When I walked past one group or another, they'd chant: *Two, four, six, eight, we ain't gonna integrate*. . . . Then they'd erupt in laughter.

Sometimes I'd feel a sharp kick in the calf or a jab in the arm as I passed them. There were a few teachers who'd step in, call out a name, and write up a disciplinary report. But many of them simply turned the other way. It was as though they didn't want to know. Because to know in good conscience might have meant having to *do* something and stand up for us. I didn't waste my breath reporting anything to them. I didn't want to face the frustration that some of my comrades faced when they tried to report violent incidents to teachers and were met with a question: Did any adult witness it? The guards, they said, didn't count.

The teachers and the guards didn't stop the verbal taunts in the halls, either, so I found my own ways of dealing with those, too. The insults were regular and plentiful, hurled from every corner of the halls like rocks—*nigger . . . baboon . . . you think you're white . . . coon.* I tried to envision the words as bubbles left floating in the air. When their words hit my ears, I'd kind of smirk to myself and think: That's all you got? But I'd be lying if I said I let them slide off me every time. Some days I just wasn't in the mood for any of it. Some days I was so mentally exhausted that I didn't have the energy to guard my heart. In those low moments, when the troublemakers hurled their insults, they smashed my spirit like bricks. It took all my energy just to stay on my feet and keep moving forward to the next class.

Class offered little solace, though. A whole new set of defense mechanisms was required there. The most common pranks usually involved my desk. A time or two, I plopped down in a puddle of spit or glue, only to look up and find several of my classmates doubled over with laughter. Humiliated, I just did what I could to wipe the stain from my clothes. But from then on, I quickly inspected my seat or ran my hand across it before sitting down. Some incidents I couldn't prevent, like the flying spitballs, blown out through a short straw. They stung my face and my neck repeatedly, and I refused to acknowledge it. At times I'd hear the sudden flick of a fountain pen, and before I could lean out of the way, a spurt of ink would ruin my clothes. I just added a change of clothes to my locker. But after the repeated break-ins of my locker, I started keeping my change of clothes in the office of Mrs. Huckaby, the vice principal.

I was always on edge in school. All nine of us were. There were two lunch shifts, and every day I sat with the other black kids who shared my lunch period. That was the only time I saw them during the school day. The usual crew included Jeff, Thelma, Ernie, and Elizabeth, but that sometimes varied. We always sat in the same spot, at the second table on the far right. I always brought my lunch from home so I could avoid the cafeteria line. None of the white kids ever invited me to join them at their tables, and the truth be told, I never even thought much about it. I looked forward to seeing my friends. It was the only time in the school day that I felt at ease enough to laugh.

By the end of each school day, the nine of us were exhausted. When we climbed into the car to head to the Bateses' home, it was the first time of the day that all nine of us were together again, and we were happy to see one another. Some of the others shared stories about what had happened to them that day. Being teenagers, we usually found a way to laugh about it. I laughed with my comrades, but I rarely chimed in on the storytelling. I just didn't want to relive any of it. Every ounce of energy I had left, I needed for homework. Sometimes, when one of us had experienced a particularly tough day, the car would fall silent. We'd notice a pair of watery eyes, and we knew. Every one of us just knew.

Once we arrived at the home of Mr. and Mrs. Bates, we'd grab a snack from the stash she kept for us in the kitchen—chips, cookies, cold drinks. We usually headed down to the basement for a casual debriefing with Mrs. Bates. Each of us found a comfortable spot on the sofa, in a chair, or on the floor to answer her questions. She would ask each of us about our day—who did what, when, where, whether we reported the trouble, whether anyone witnessed it, and who, if anyone, responded. At first, I dutifully told her all that I had experienced. But day after day, nothing seemed to change. I know she would have fixed it if she could have, but it seemed to me that she was about as helpless to fix things as we were. So I stopped sharing. For some, those sessions may have been cathartic. For me, it was wasted breath, wasted energy, having to go through the trauma all over again. When my turn to share rolled around, I'd just say, "My day was all right" or "Things went okay." At home, I'd respond the same way when my parents or younger sisters asked about my day. I didn't want to worry them any more than I already had.

At the end of the first grading period, a reporter for a national newspaper called Mrs. Huckaby to ask how we nine were doing academically. It seemed the whole world was waiting to see if we could keep up with the white students. That was confidential information, Mrs. Huckaby responded, but added that the reporter should check the following Sunday's newspaper, when the *Arkansas Gazette* listed the students who had made the honor roll. My name was on the list. Despite all the distractions, I somehow had managed to focus enough on my studies to make it.

My eight comrades and I still had a military escort throughout the day at Central. The military continued to meet us at the home of Mr. and Mrs. Bates and drive us to school every day until late October, when a few of our parents started carpooling.

Much of the kicking, punching, spitting, shoving, and shoulder bumping continued at school. The more the teachers were on the lookout, the more the trouble-makers got better at hiding their dirty deeds. Things at Central were still turbulent in mid-November when the *Gazette* assigned a team of reporters to scope out daily life at the school. The resulting story didn't even come close to capturing the truth. Much of it was based on rumors and factual inaccuracies, including a teacher who reported to her class that all nine of us would be leaving at Thanksgiving. The story also described a white girl spitting on an unnamed black girl—all of which was witnessed by a teacher, who looked away.

But I was most furious when I read this ridiculous attack: One white girl complained, "They dress sloppy. . . .

They wear colored socks. No white girl would think of wearing anything but white socks."

With all that was going on, it might have been easy to lose sight of the fact that we were, after all, teenagers. What we wore to school mattered to us, as did what others thought of what we wore. My mother made most of my clothes, and I looked good. My clothes were neat and stylish. In fact, all nine of us were well-groomed—our clothes always clean, perfectly pressed, and fashionable.

The *Gazette* story summarized the first three months of integration at Central this way: "not entirely calm . . . but not in turmoil either." Perhaps that was the view from the outside peeking in. From the center of the drama, it sure felt like turmoil to me.

On the other side, Mrs. Bates and the NAACP were just as determined to spin the story the other way—that integration was working perfectly well, which was less than the truth. All nine of us felt compelled to send out that unified message—that integration was succeeding.

I had heard all my life both at home and at school that I was a representative not only of my family but of the entire race. White folks would forever judge the race by what each of us said and did, my parents and teachers had told me. Likewise, Mrs. Bates said, white folks would judge how well integration was working by what the nine of us said and did. It was as if we bore all the responsibility for the success or failure of integration. So I did what

I believed was expected. I played down my suffering. The message that Mrs. Bates drilled in us rang constantly in my ears:

"This is important. It is history. You are helping to change the way America thinks about our race."

The rational part of me understood the huge significance of that. But at times, the other part—the fourteen-year-old girl who just wanted to go to school without all the drama—felt used. That was the part of me that came to resent the media interviews we were asked to do.

It got even more difficult as the months passed to keep from fighting back. One particular redhead made restraint especially difficult for me.

I got caught up in the crush of the hallway crowd between classes one day, which slowed my stride. With so many people around me in every direction, it didn't seem unusual at first that someone was walking so closely behind me, directly in my tracks. Then all of a sudden, a shoe crunched down hard on the back of my right heel. A sharp pain shot up the back of my leg. The person behind me must have been in a rush, I first thought. I walked faster. The person behind me sped up, too. And then, crunch—it happened again. And again. I heard laughter behind me. This was deliberate.

I could see the red hair in my peripheral vision, and she was purposely walking on my heels. This time, the pain was intense, like a big razor blade dragged from the back of my lower ankle down to my heel. I wanted to cry out, but I sucked it in and tried to move faster. Eventually, she shot from behind me to head to her class, and I saw her—a bit shorter than me at about five feet seven inches tall, with milky skin and straight, shoulder-length red hair pulled into a ponytail. I didn't recognize her from any of my classes. I kept walking, trying to block from my mind what had just happened as I continued to my next class. The back of my ankle and heel felt raw rubbing against my sock and shoe. It wasn't until later that afternoon in the gym locker room that I was able to inspect my heel without showing that I was hurt. I peeled back my sock. Spots of blood had soaked through. I felt the tears rising from my throat, but I choked them back, pulled up my sock, and headed out to the gym. I'd have to remember to bring Band-Aids next time.

The redhead became one of my regular tormentors in the halls. She'd wait for me almost every day, usually after lunch, and before I knew it, she was on my heels. I walked as fast as I could in those crowded halls. If she was going to rip the skin off my heels, I'd make her work for it. I told Mrs. Bates about it. Nothing changed. Then, one day in one of my low moments, instinct kicked in. The same girl skirted up behind me to start her routine, and instead of speeding up, I stopped dead in my tracks. She slammed into me. I whipped around to face her. I could tell that she was surprised. I wanted to sock her but thought better of it. I stared her down and let my eyes do the talking. Other students stared and walked around us. She hissed and scampered away. That turned out to be a rather good day.

I wish I could say that was the end of the heel walking, but the redhead was soon back at it. Sometimes, others followed suit. Occasionally, I reported the incidents. A female student I didn't know who tried to trip me as I entered the cafeteria. Or the boys who purposely bumped into me hard enough to spin me around. Mostly, I just did what I could to avoid them and stay on guard.

One day, being on guard had a surprising result. As I headed to class, I noticed five or six of the black-leather clan in my path ahead. I knew that one of them would slink next to me and throw out an elbow as I passed. I came up with a quick plan: I'd throw out my own elbow to block it. I'd have to time it just right. Inching closer, I carefully moved my books to the right, next to the guard, to free my left arm. On cue, one of the boys stepped out of the group and took a couple of steps next to me. This time, I was ready. I threw out my elbow to protect myself before feeling his blow. For some reason, though, his elbow hadn't moved, and to his astonishment—and mine—he felt the sharp point of my elbow jab into his arm. He jumped back.

"You see what that nigger did to me!" he yelled, red-faced.

I kept walking, hoping that the teachers monitoring the halls at that moment were as blind as they had been all the times I'd been tortured in those same halls. Fortunately, I never heard anything about it. But one of my comrades wouldn't be so lucky.

It was December 17, the day before Christmas break. When I walked up to the lunch table, I noticed that Ernie looked more frustrated than usual. He threw his books and lunch sack on the table. Minnijean was in trouble, he said. She'd dumped a big bowl of chili on the head of a boy who had been hassling her repeatedly in the lunch line. He and Melba had seen it all: A group of boys called Minnie names and blocked her path as she tried to make her way to her table with her lunch. Before Ernie could tell her to ignore them, he said, he watched the chili slide from Minnie's tilted tray onto the boy's head. The entire cafeteria came to a standstill for a moment, and spontaneously, the black cafeteria staff erupted in applause. An administrator whisked Minnie to the main office. Ernie said he hadn't seen Minnie since. The word was she'd been suspended.

I felt awful for Minnie. She had been pushed to the breaking point, and I knew that it easily could have been any one of us. We were all tired of life in the pressure cooker, and at one time or another, every one of us had felt one notch away from blowing. I nibbled on my sandwich for the rest of lunch. None of us felt much like talking. We were worried about what this would mean for Minnie, what it would mean for us all.

I learned later that Minnie had been suspended and would have to reapply for admission when we returned from Christmas break in January. The news put a damper on the beginning of the two-week break from school, but I looked forward to the time off. Finally, I would be able to let down my guard, laugh freely, and enjoy my family and friends. Two days before Christmas, I did exactly that when the nine of us and our parents gathered at the Dunbar Community Center for a huge holiday celebration in our honor. The large upstairs room sparkled with festive lights and decorations. I wore a red-and-white taffeta dress in a polka-dot print. It was especially nice to see Mother and Daddy dressed in their holiday finery, enjoying themselves like old times. Before Central, they often got all spruced up for a night on the town, but much of the fun in their lives as a young couple now seemed to have dried up. I missed the laughter that had been present in our home.

Near the end of the party, a Santa presented each of us with gifts and encouraging letters mailed from around the country, thanking us for our bravery and courage. I'll never forget that evening. It came at a particularly low point and reminded us all that no matter how isolated we sometimes felt at Central, we were not in this fight alone.

As 1957 wound to a close, I realized just how much of the world was watching us. I picked up the *Gazette* one day and saw a story that said the Associated Press had ranked the Little Rock Nine and our integration battle as the top story of the year in the nation—even bigger than the passage of the Civil Rights Act, the first major civil rights legislation since Reconstruction.

All too soon, the holidays were over and school was back in session. I had but one wish for the new year: that life at Central would somehow get easier. But it didn't take long for that wish to fizzle. On the first day of school after Christmas break, classes were interrupted for what students had been told was a fire drill. It seemed strange when the police department showed up and began searching inside, but we later learned that a bomb threat had been made against the school. Such threats would become almost a routine part of our day.

I soon learned to take my coat with me when we left the building, because I knew it'd be at least a half-hour wait. While standing outside, the white students rolled their eyes or cut mean looks at the black students, as if we were causing this inconvenience.

In late January, a search did not come up empty. Dynamite had been found in an unused locker. Superintendent Blossom maintained that the bomb threats were just a scare tactic intended to force school officials to close Central.

The next day, another anonymous caller phoned in a threat—this time to the *Arkansas Gazette*. The operator described the caller as a "white boy who had muffled his voice." A frustrated Blossom pleaded in the newspaper and on television for citizens to act responsibly and stop this disruption to the academic process. But his words fell on deaf ears, because the threats, the searches, and the long waits in the cold continued. Bomb parts were found, but none that seemed to pose a real threat.

However, the message from the segregationists was clear: They were not backing off. If anything, they felt even more emboldened by Minnie's suspension. Minnie returned to school in mid-January, and the attacks on her were relentless. One of the tormentors drenched her with hot soup. She didn't respond, but the taunts continued daily. On the morning of February 6, Minnie had taken enough and retorted by calling a student "white trash," which got her suspended again and ultimately expelled from Central for good.

Mrs. Bates somehow got a copy of a confidential school record dubbed "Students Involved in Repeated Incidents at Central High School," which noted some of the harassment. The report shows that 1958 was already off to a very rocky start:

James Cole sacked Ernie in the shower with scalding

hot towels and used abusive language; James also called Minnijean a "nigger-looking bitch" and refused to go to the principal's office when the guard ordered him to do so.

Darlene Holloway stepped on Melba's heels and pushed Elizabeth down the stairs.

Lester Judkins pretended Ernie tripped him after Kenneth Vandiver struck Ernie.

These were just a few of the incidents that made the list, and most times, I didn't even bother reporting them. My days were so stressful that I didn't entirely feel bad for Minnijean now that she was expelled: At least she was free from the troubles at Central.

Mrs. Bates and the NAACP arranged for her to move to New York and live with Drs. Kenneth and Mamie Clark, the renowned African American psychologists whose research using black and white dolls showed the devastating effects of racism and segregation on black children. The findings had been essential to the success of the Supreme Court's *Brown* decision. They lived in Hastings-on-Hudson, a New York City suburb nestled among the hills along the Hudson River, which sounded exotic and exciting. The couple helped Minnie attain a scholarship to the prestigious New Lincoln School in New York.

The remaining eight of us, our parents, and Mrs. Bates went to the airport to see Minnijean off. She was about to fly off into what seemed to me a much brighter future and a wonderful adventure. I felt more excited for her than sad. A link in our chain had been snapped off, but Minnie no longer had to carry the burden of Central. I put myself in her place and wondered what it would be like to fly far away from friends and family and live with famous strangers. The cold wind whistled as we stood near the tarmac, saying our goodbyes. We waved and waved as Minnijean turned and walked away, her face reflecting what we all felt—excitement and regret. One of the guys broke into a verse of the song "You Can Make It If You Try."

No sooner had Minnijean left Central than hateful cards began appearing all over the school: ONE DOWN ... EIGHT TO GO. Distributing the cards led to the suspension of one perennial troublemaker, Sammy Dean Parker. Another card was aimed at Gloria: GET GLORIA RAY—OUT OF THE WAY. Even the principal, Jess Matthews, was a target: THAT WHITE TRASH MATTHEWS NAMED JESS / SURE GOT CENTRAL IN A MESS / THE KIDS—IF THEY'RE WHITE / HE DEPRIVES OF THEIR RIGHTS / HE'S A KANSAS NIGGER-LOVER, I GUESS.

We knew, too, that the troublemakers were organized in their campaign to punish us physically. One of the cards found around school invited white students to attack us: GOOD ONLY UNTIL MAY 29, 1958 / BEARER MAY KICK RUMPS OF EACH CHS NEGRO ONCE PER DAY UNTIL ABOVE EXPIRATION DATE / LAST CHANCE, BOYS. DO NOT USE SPIKED SHOES ...

Practically everywhere I walked, I felt like one big bull's-eye. That's exactly how I felt at lunchtime on March 12 as I headed down the school stairs and suddenly felt a round, wet blob smash against me. I had been hit by a tomato. From the second-floor landing, I quickly looked up and saw the guilty party, one of the smirking black-leather boys. I felt both furious and humiliated as I headed to Mrs. Huckaby's office to change clothes. Tomato dripped from a huge stain on my skirt and blouse.

There was, however, one place on campus where I could go without feeling that I was such a target: chapel. It was really just a large classroom, filled with desks and chairs, on the main level of the school. But for about twenty minutes each morning before classes began, the classroom became a place of meditation and prayer. I started each school day there. On any given morning, about thirty white students also attended. There was no interaction between the black and white students, but I knew that at least we had come there for a common purpose: to pray. Mr. Ivy usually asked the white students to lead the program, which generally included a Bible reading, prayer, and hymns—my favorite part of the service, especially the old standard "Amazing Grace." I could often hear Melba's—or, before she left, Minnijean's—melodic voice rising above the crowd. This became my haven, the place where I found the spiritual fuel I needed to get through each day.

Sometimes I've thought about how much easier survival would have been if more people had taken a stand. As I saw it, the students at Central fell into different categories. The smallest group was the easiest to identify, those students who were determined to make our lives miserable. They were the tormentors, the ones who called us hateful slurs, spat on us, kicked, hit, pushed, and slammed us into lockers and down the stairs. Maybe it was their parents out there in the segregationist crowds, clinging to the wrongheaded belief that Central somehow belonged to them and that we nine were intruders causing trouble by having the audacity to keep showing up.

The second group included students who were sympathetic, though they did not outwardly show it or jump to our defense in times of trouble. You could tell by the kind eyes that on our worst days seemed to say: "I'm really sorry this is happening to you." Sometimes, they offered a shy smile in the hallways or in class or slipped a quiet note of support to one of us undercover. Gloria has talked fondly about Becky, a white girl with whom she exchanged notes during one of her classes. In their notes, Becky and Gloria established a sort of friendship. On paper, they were just girls who shared the same interests, but the parameters of their relationship were clear. When Gloria wrote one day to ask whether she should speak if she saw Becky in the halls, Becky responded: "No, please don't." She didn't want to be dubbed by the loud-mouthed segregationists a "nigger-lover."

The majority of students at Central fell into the third group: those who kept silent. They wanted all the "trouble" to end. They did not torment us, but they didn't extend any kindness to us in any way, either, not even quietly. They did not want to be associated with one side or the other. They chose to remain neutral—as if remaining neutral in the face of evil were an acceptable choice. They are most likely the ones today who, when asked about the Class of 1957, try to reinvent history. Things at Central weren't as bad as the nine of us have said, they claimed in later years. The mobs weren't as big, they say, the bad guys and gals weren't as bad, and the atmosphere wasn't as tense. Well, of course that is how they remember the Central journey fifty-plus years later. When I was suffering in those hallowed halls, they turned away. They did nothing. They said nothing. They *chose* not to see.

There was one other group, a small group, for sure, but in my mind the bravest of all: those teachers and students who at times were openly kind, who seemed to look beyond skin color and see nine students eager to learn, eager to be part of a great academic institution. Mr. Bell, my biology teacher, was one of them. He was young, but he seemed worldly and wise. He had fought in the Korean War and had seen life far beyond Little Rock. He kept an eye on me in class and kept the troublemakers at bay. He even encouraged me to participate in the science fair. He chose to see me.

There were others, too. The yearbook from my tenth-grade year includes kind notes from more than a dozen white classmates who risked harassment for taking even that small step. Their words will forever remind me that there were moments in the midst of chaos when black and white faded and we were just teenagers. Liz Dolan, whose locker was a few away from mine, wrote in my yearbook:

> Dear Carlotta,
>     This has been a memorable year for all of us—just wish you didn't have so many un-happy ones. Remember I am for you. Good luck to a really great girl. . . .

Then there was Jenny Lee Ball, a dark-haired girl who always wore her shoulder-length hair pulled back in a ponytail. She was on the student council, and we also shared gym. Whenever Jenny was team captain, she always chose me. My name wasn't the first one Jenny called, and neither was it the last. And there wasn't a hint of scorn or regret when she boldly called out my name. When our team got into the huddle to discuss our gym-nastics formation Jenny included me in the discussion. What was I good at? Where should I fit? I remember

Jenny as befriending me, though I can't think of a specific thing she said or did that was particularly special. But I guess that was the point. I saw nothing in her eyes and heard nothing in her tone that suggested she thought I was special or different. She treated me with the same consideration and dignity she showed everybody else. That's all I ever really wanted. That's all every one of us wanted.

And each time I encountered a rare soul who seemed to recognize that, I considered it a real blessing.

# CHAPTER 7

## Star-Studded Summer

**W**hen the segregationists failed to force the remaining eight of us out of Central, they began targeting our parents. And they hit where it hurt—our parents' pockets and pocketbooks.

I first noticed that something strange was going on with my father when he began arriving home from work in the middle of the day on a regular basis. More and more often, when I made it home from school, Daddy was already there. Before, he had rarely made it home before supper.

During the spring of 1958, Daddy landed a job as a subcontractor on a new grocery store chain opening in Little Rock. He was hopeful because this was a major construction job expected to last for months. That meant steady work and steady income. For his first day on the job, he left home around sunrise, as usual. But when I returned from school that day, he was already home. He and Mother were deep in conversation in their bedroom.

"They laid me off," I heard him say.

It had happened again. Daddy would get a job, and then a few hours or a few days later, he would be told for no apparent reason that his services were no longer needed. Daddy was a meticulous brick mason. He had never had trouble finding or keeping work—until now. I knew this had to be part of the segregationists' scheme to punish him and anyone else involved in the integration of Central. They had already targeted the *Arkansas Gazette*, the local newspaper that had featured editorials supporting integration with the argument that it was the law of the land. The newspaper's coverage of the events at Central seemed more balanced than that of its local competitor, the *Arkansas Democrat*, which favored segregation. But to the segregationists, there was no middle ground and no such thing as neutral; the *Gazette* was the enemy. Only months earlier, during the Christmas season, segregationists had also boycotted any businesses that advertised in the paper, just to make the paper lose money and shut down.

Meanwhile, I'd heard talk among my comrades that some of their parents had lost jobs, too. Jefferson's father was laid off from his longtime job at International Harvester, which manufactured construction equipment. The mothers of Gloria and Elizabeth were also laid off.

They all suffered quietly, but when Melba's mother, Lois Pattillo, was informed that she was laid off from her job as a seventh-grade English teacher, she bravely decided to go public with her struggle. Mrs. Pattillo, who was the family's sole breadwinner, wrote a statement and called the newspapers. On May 7, the *Gazette* ran her story on the front page, and it was picked up by media around the world. The resulting publicity ultimately helped Mrs. Pattillo get her job back.

My father wasn't quite as fortunate. He still could not land a decent contract in Arkansas. My grandfathers helped out as much as they could. Grandpa Cullins mostly took small jobs as the primary contractor on construction projects for black churches, schools, and businesses. That allowed him to sidestep the racists, and he was able to hire Daddy to work for him. Big Daddy also gave Daddy more work hours in the café/pool hall. And Mother went back to work. Still, my parents were struggling financially. Mother began paying more attention to price tags in the grocery store and buying just the essentials. The occasional splurges on clothing and out-of-town trips also came to a halt.

Then, one day my parents told me that Daddy would be going to Los Angeles, California, for the summer to work. He had heard that plenty of good-paying construction jobs were available there. The news was bittersweet. I was happy that Daddy, who took such pride in his work, finally would be able to do the kind of work he enjoyed and make the money he deserved. But I would miss him. When Daddy was away for even a day, I always felt less secure.

Ernie's graduation helped to take my mind off Daddy's departure. I was so proud of my friend. His graduation said to the world that even under the most extreme circumstances, black students could perform as well as any others. Ernie had persevered through a nightmare that only the nine of us knew, and he'd completed all but this final walk across the stage. I wanted to be there to support him and was disappointed to learn that I would not be allowed to attend. As expected, there had been a higher than usual number of threats. In such a volatile atmosphere, anything could happen.

On May 27, thousands of parents, guests, and school officials gathered at Quigley Stadium for the big event. Hundreds of National Guard troops were there, too, and practically every police officer and detective on the Little Rock force. I gathered with my family in the den just before eight p.m. to listen to a radio broadcast of the ceremony. That familiar knot in my stomach tightened as I listened, hoping that those with hateful intentions wouldn't ruin Ernie's special night. Governor Faubus and his crew of die-hard segregationists already had proclaimed the first year of integration at Central a dismal failure. Who knew if one of those loonies would make it a self-fulfilled prophecy with some final, awful act?

Ernie was among 602 graduates to receive their diplomas that night. About fifty minutes into the ceremony, his name was called. It seemed as though all of Little Rock—maybe even the entire nation—was holding its breath. There was not a sound. No laughter, no cheers, no applause, none of the celebratory expressions that had accompanied the names of all the other graduates. Just silence. I exhaled as I imagined Ernie proudly walking across that stage—the first student of color ever to do so. Surely, all those ghosts of our black ancestral history—those unnamed warriors who'd risked torture by white slave owners to learn the words in Bibles and books, who'd braved the whips and the snarling dogs, and in some cases died without ever reaching brighter shores—surely, they were helping to lift his head and straighten his shoulders now.

The media also took note of one special guest who had attended the graduation with Ernie's family: Reverend Martin Luther King, Jr. At the time, Dr. King was clearly on the rise. He had achieved acclaim as leader of the successful Montgomery bus boycott, but he had not yet reached the legendary status that would come in the years ahead. He was just another man in the crowd. The mention of Dr. King in the newspaper made me flash back to the first time I met him. He had come to Little Rock to speak and was staying at the home of Mr. and Mrs. Bates, who invited the nine of us to meet him. I brought along my friend Bunny, and meeting Dr. King remains one of the highlights of her life.

Dr. King's presence spoke to the significance of Ernie's graduation. Now, for Ernie, Central was history. He was heading to Michigan State University in the fall. For me, Central was history, too—at least for a while. Summer had officially arrived, and not a moment too soon.

Within days of Ernie's graduation, the eight of us took a plane to Chicago to be honored by the *Chicago Defender*. It was the first plane ride for most of us. Minnijean met us there, and we were all thrilled to see her again and to vacation together for several days in this city we all had read about but had never seen.

We stayed downtown in an integrated hotel. Gloria and I roomed together, Minnie and Melba, Elizabeth and Thelma, and the three guys. The newspaper honored the nine of us with the Robert Sengstacke Abbott Award, named for the founder and editor of the *Chicago Defender*, who was the most successful black newspaper publisher of his era. He had been an early advocate of civil rights and had encouraged colored men and women in the South to move north to pursue a better life. The banquet in our honor was held at the glamorous Morrison Hotel. All of us were overwhelmed by the grandeur of the place but even more by the size and enthusiasm of the crowd. More than five hundred people gathered in the Cameo Ballroom, and all to see us. In Little Rock, we had drawn crowds for sure. Here, people stood to their feet to applaud us. They called us brave and told us we were heroes and that they had been pulling for us. For the first time, it really hit me—the magnitude, the scope, of what the nine of us had done. It wasn't just about each of us having access to the best education available in Little Rock. It was about parting once-closed doors for children of color everywhere. It was about the generations to come.

John Sengstacke, editor of the *Chicago Defender* and nephew of the newspaper's founder, invited us to his summer home in Michigan City, Indiana, about an hour from downtown Chicago. There, we were entertained royally, with activities that included a boat ride on the family's private lake. In those few days, the nine of us shared more laughter and fun than we had the entire year at Central. We felt like teenagers again, carefree and silly, not nine symbols to be either admired or loathed. Little did we know this was only the first stop in what would be a star-studded summer.

In July, we took another plane ride, this time to Cleveland. The NAACP was awarding us its prestigious Spingarn Medal, presented for outstanding achievement. The award was named for Joel Elias Spingarn, a lifelong civil rights advocate, one of the early white leaders and later board chairman of the NAACP. Spingarn's desire was to draw attention to the distinguished achievements of African Americans with an award that would inspire the ambitions of young people. Mrs. Bates and the nine of us were the first and still the only group ever to receive it. I still feel extremely humbled to be mentioned among the great men and women who had also been recipients, including W. E. B. Du Bois, George Washington Carver, Charles Chesnutt, Mary McLeod Bethune, Marian Anderson, Thurgood Marshall, and Jackie Robinson. In 1957, the year before we received the award, it was presented to Dr. Martin Luther King, Jr.

Before leaving the city, we were treated to dinner at the legendary Dearing's Restaurant, known for its "Original Golden Brown Fried Chicken." The popular restaurant served food that reminded me of home: ribs, shrimp, homemade rolls, and pastries. It was comfort food, but this was a well-appointed, black-owned restaurant (complete with white linen tablecloths) that also drew white residents of the city. Like my childhood summer in New York, these experiences opened the gates to a life far more progressive and sophisticated than anything I had ever experienced in Little Rock.

Soon enough, we were next off to New York for a whirlwind tour with Mrs. Bates, which had been generously sponsored by the AFL-CIO Hotel Employees

Union #6—working-class people, like ourselves. First stop was the office of Roy Wilkins, executive secretary of the NAACP, one of the early civil rights leaders I'd learned about at Dunbar. In his presence, I was a starstruck fifteen-year-old, watching a figure I'd read about suddenly come to life. Later, we met New York mayor Robert F. Wagner, Jr., and Governor W. Averell Harriman, and attended a fundraiser in Harlem, where Thurgood Marshall and Adam Clayton Powell were also guests.

Honestly, by then, most of us were a bit tired of being paraded around. As proud as we were, I think all of us were just overwhelmed by the attention and unsure how to handle this new spotlight.

One of the most memorable, down-to-earth evenings in New York was hosted by Drs. Kenneth and Mamie Clark, the psychologists who had taken in Minnijean when she was expelled from Central. They had a lovely home at Hastings-on-Hudson, and Broadway stars Ossie Davis and Ruby Dee were waiting to meet us there. They had children our age and talked to us like nurturing, protective parents, inquiring about our well-being.

Later, we went to see David Merrick's new Broadway play, *Jamaica*, starring Lena Horne and Ricardo Montalban. We got to meet the other actors backstage after the show. I loved Lena Horne. She was warm and engaging, not to mention stunning. I knew little then about her politics—how she had refused to perform for segregated audiences during World War II, how her friendship with outspoken activist and actor Paul Robeson had left her branded a Communist and blacklisted in Hollywood in the 1950s, how she again and again aligned herself with civil rights causes. But the more I learned about Lena Horne in the ensuing years, the more I admired her. After the show that night, I only knew that I felt a connection to her, perhaps because she reminded me so much of my mother. The way Ms. Horne carried herself—the way she threw her shawl around her shoulders with the grace of an onstage performance—that sure enough was Mother.

After meeting with the performers, we and our adult chaperones ended the evening at Lindy's restaurant, a popular hangout for Broadway stars. There, like everywhere we went, the staff catered to us as though we were stars, too. It astounded me that day after day we met internationally renowned entertainers and politicians, yet they treated us as if *we* were the celebrities. It felt unreal and at times, for me, a bit uncomfortable.

And then our glorious week was done.

I didn't head back to Little Rock just yet, though. Gloria and I were going to separate summer camps in the New York area. Thanks to a generous sponsor, I was sent to Camp Minisink, a wooded campsite in the Shawangunk Mountains of New York. The New York City Mission Society ran the camp, which offered youths, mostly from

Harlem, the chance to experience the outdoors and nature far away from the concrete city.

Camp Minisink was similar to the Y-Teen sessions I'd attended at Camp Clearfork in the Ouachita Mountains of Arkansas, but on a grander scale. Everything, it seemed, was larger—the lake, which flowed as far as the eye could see, and the woods, which spanned more than six hundred acres. But at Camp Clearfork, all the campers were primarily teenage girls of color. At Minisink, we were a mix of boys and girls, middle class and poor, Latin American and black. Our days and evenings were spent doing typical outdoor camp activities—hiking, boating, playing games, competing, cooking, cleaning, and singing around the campfire. We took turns bussing our meal tables and swapping pieces of our dialects and culture. My friends used to laugh at how I said "water." I guess I subconsciously threw in an extra "r," as in "warter." And my new northern buddies just found that hilarious. I, of course, had no idea what was so funny because I've never had much of a southern accent—at least, I've never thought so. But I had my share of fun, too, with their dialects from Puerto Rico, the West Indian islands, and those other worlds within the U.S. borders—Miami and the Bronx.

For the first time, I was learning about foods I'd never tasted, trying out dances I'd never seen, and hearing stories about how other kids lived. The other campers all knew my story, and some were naturally curious. But they didn't pester me with questions about Central. I was just one of them. At the time, I couldn't adequately express what a balm Camp Minisink had been for my bruised psyche, but I felt it deep in my bones. Finally, my soul and spirit could rest.

Soon it was time to say goodbye to my Minisink friends. On our last night was a social. This time we were not in camp clothes, but dressed up. And we got to display on the dance floor all the new moves we had bragged about and occasionally demonstrated on those sweaty days in the woods.

I left Camp Minisink knowing that I had made some lifelong friends.

There was just one more stop for me before I returned to Little Rock. My eight Little Rock comrades and I had been invited to Washington, DC, to attend the Elks convention, an annual event. After those wonderful weeks in New York, a city that was a true melting pot, Washington felt more like being back in Little Rock. In the stores, on the streets, in the hotel, we were segregated. People of different races lived separately. This was shocking to me. I hadn't expected it in the nation's capital.

The nine of us were scheduled to be in a DC parade—a long, big one with a specially designed float just for us. We smiled big for the cameras and waved to the crowds.

Melba and Minnie especially loved the parade. I hated it. I felt embarrassed—embarrassed that we were such spectacles. I knew the Elks meant well by honoring us, and they even presented each of us with a $1,000 scholarship. I was hugely grateful for that truly generous gift that helped to relieve our worries about how we would pay for college. But I guess after a month of fun as just another teenager at camp, I wasn't eager to return to the spotlight associated with Central High School.

The time in Washington marked the end of summer break, which had felt like a little slice of heaven. Now it was time to head back to Little Rock and Central. All the way home, I was filled with dread. I knew what awaited me there.

I was returning to hell.

# CHAPTER 8

## Just a Matter of Time

**M**y junior year at Central hadn't even started yet when the legal fight over integration began once again. The school board was determined to call integration a failure so they could once again force school segregation. They went to court over the summer to try to change course—essentially to kick out us black students. While the nine of us were being hailed as heroes throughout the country, the board began its push to return us to the all-black Horace Mann. There were new threats of violence, the school board told the court, and the citizens of Little Rock needed more time to adjust to integration. They planned to delay integration until January 1961. I wondered: Why do we have to be punished for other people's violence and bad behavior? Why aren't the authorities and politicians calling out the people kicking up trouble instead of cowing to them and making us pay the price?

Instead of the heroic Judge Ronald Davies, the case was assigned to an Arkansas federal judge. On June 21, U.S. District judge Harry Lemley granted the school board's request for a delay. Until that moment, the segregationists had been losing; now it felt like the clock would start ticking backward. The NAACP immediately appealed to the court to overturn the decision to delay integration.

Thurgood Marshall returned with Wiley Branton to represent us. It was a relief when we heard that Marshall had won the day, and the appellate court reversed Judge Lemley's ruling.

But what happened next was a series of bewildering events.

The school board still refused to give in to integration, and it appealed to the U.S. Supreme Court. When the new school year rolled around on September 2, 1958—the usual Tuesday after Labor Day—the city's four high schools remained closed. Once again, I was sitting at home in limbo, waiting for the nation's highest court to rule on the future of integration in Little Rock.

Ten days later, the Supreme Court spoke. Chief Justice Earl Warren ordered the Little Rock school district to proceed with integration, and let kids go to school already.

But Governor Faubus counteracted, sneakily. By the time the Supreme Court had issued its order, he had already called a special session of the state legislature. There, he pushed through six anti-integration bills, which gave him extraordinary powers over the school system. Just hours after the Supreme Court announcement, Governor Faubus made his stunning move: He signed the anti-integration bills into law and utilized his new power: to shut down all three public high schools in Little Rock.

And just like that, thirty-seven hundred students, black and white, were left wondering: What now?

The news infuriated me. Governor Faubus strutted before television cameras to justify his decision, as if upsetting the lives of so many people were a perfectly normal thing to do. How dared he jeopardize the futures of thousands of students? How was I going to complete my junior year now? Ernie had left for Michigan State, Minnijean was back in New York, and the parents of two of my other comrades had decided already that their families would take no more. They had already walked through hell and had no intention of looking back. Terry and his family moved to Los Angeles, leaving Little Rock for good. Gloria and her mother relocated around the same time to Kansas City, Missouri, while her father maintained the family home in Little Rock. That left Jefferson, Elizabeth, Thelma, Melba, and me.

Mrs. Bates did her best to try to reassure us and our parents while we waited for the school year to finally begin.

We could take correspondence courses—essentially remote learning—through the University of Arkansas, she told us. And in the meantime, she promised, the NAACP would continue to fight for us.

My own feelings were mixed, just as they had been when Minnijean first left for New York. I was sad that those of us who had been through so much together at Central wouldn't be able to finish our journey together. But I was happy that my comrades were moving on to more peaceful lives. Five of the nine—Terry, Minnie, Melba, Elizabeth, and Thelma—were seniors now.

Through it all, though, my family never even talked about leaving Little Rock—at least, as far as I knew. Perhaps to my parents, the idea of leaving their families and everything they had ever known was scarier than the prospect of facing another uncertain year at Central. While the thought of going to school in another city at times seemed tempting and adventurous, I felt a strong need to stay close to my parents and sisters. I felt guilty because I saw how much my family was struggling, and I knew it was because of my decision to attend Central. With Daddy having trouble earning a steady paycheck, Mother had gotten a job working for the city. I wanted to do my part, so I took on the responsibility of caring for Tina, who was three years old.

Families like mine weren't the only ones suddenly scrambling after the school closings to figure out what to do. The school board also had to keep teachers from quitting the system en masse. To quell the teachers' fears, the board agreed to continue paying them. Then, when an uproar rose from the community over the prospect of a year without football, the board (with the support of the governor) made provisions for the season to continue. So even though thousands of families were scurrying to find academic alternatives for their children, teachers were reporting to empty classrooms, and the football teams practiced and played a regular schedule.

Even though my parents were struggling financially, they were determined to keep me on track academically. They scraped up the extra money to pay for the remote learning courses and rent the textbooks. So, too, did the families of Jefferson, Elizabeth, Thelma, and Melba, who also took the courses. There were no computers then, so everything was done on paper and mailed over to us. The Dunbar Community Center arranged for students in the community who wanted to do our schoolwork together to meet there every day and get help from retired teachers and volunteers from the local library.

Every day, Mother dropped Tina and me off at the center, as though we were going to school. For half a day, I did my correspondence work. My first two courses were U.S. History II and English II, and the assignments came in white folders from the University of Arkansas in Fayetteville. Twenty-four assignments were enclosed in each packet, but I was instructed to complete no more than four per week. I quickly found that those four assignments didn't amount to nearly enough work to keep my mind occupied. Several times, I received a bright yellow slip of paper notifying me that because of increased enrollment in the courses, I was being assigned a new teacher. That happened so frequently that it was hard to keep up with who—if anyone—was seriously evaluating my work. Except for the occasional correction of a misspelled word or a brief question asking for additional information, the teacher rarely made notes on my papers. Most times, the only indication that anyone had even looked at my assignment was a grade at the top of the page. After I had completed the required two dozen assignments, an examination was mailed to me, and my grade was based on my proficiency on the test.

In many ways, those days felt empty. It just didn't make sense that we had to go so out of our way to learn and have a normal school social life. I do, however, look back fondly on the fun. On a typical day, about ten to fifteen students showed up, and it was good to be engaged with other teenagers. I missed learning, but I didn't miss the stress or isolation I'd experienced the first year at Central. At the center, most of us were done with our serious work by lunchtime, and we whiled away the afternoons at the card table. I'd hold Tina on my lap as we played checkers, dominoes, and Scrabble. We teenagers talked a lot of noise and often spelled words we thought the little one shouldn't hear. But Tina, ever a quick study, not only picked up a lifelong love for board games, she also quickly became a master speller. You could just see that wheel twirling in her brain as she tried to figure out what she was not supposed to hear. It became almost a game to her to outsmart the big kids and then blurt out our disguised words.

Despite the fun, I knew I was supposed to be in school, and I couldn't help worrying about my future, about how much my chances of getting into a good college would be hurt by these long months out of school.

Meanwhile, throughout Little Rock, the city's economy was suffering. Much of white Little Rock blamed Mrs. Bates and our parents for the crisis, including Faubus and a group calling itself the Save Our Schools Committee. In mid-September 1958, the group began running a series of newspaper ads, encouraging black ministers and other black community leaders to "appeal to Mrs. Bates and seven parents to give us time to accept this change in a Christian manner." It never ceased to amaze me how often the bigots tried to hide their fear and hatred behind the banner of Christianity.

I also started to see stories on television and in the newspapers about another group of white women calling themselves the Women's Emergency Committee to

Open Our Schools (WEC). "We stand neither for integration nor for segregation, but for education," they stated.

As I watched much of this unfold in the newspapers and on television, I changed my mind about staying in Little Rock. I was tired of the politics. I just wanted to be in school, even if it meant moving to another city for a while. Besides, by the beginning of the year, I had completed all the remote courses I could take in one semester, and I was seriously bored.

I heard that Mrs. Bates had sent out an appeal asking NAACP supporters in other cities to take in black Little Rock students interested in relocating to finish their high school education. One such offer came from a white couple in Santa Rosa, California, who were dedicated to racial justice and wanted to become a surrogate family to a displaced black student. Mrs. Bates arranged for Melba to move to the West Coast to live with the couple and their four children. I also began hearing about Horace Mann students who were being placed in other homes throughout the country.

Soon enough, in late March 1959, Mrs. Bates called to tell my parents that Dr. Nathan Christopher, an NAACP board member in Cleveland, had invited a Little Rock student to stay with his family and finish high school there. Mother and Daddy discussed it and agreed that the time may have come for me to go away to school. Of course, for me the decision was easy. By the beginning of April, I was off to Cleveland for a new adventure.

I liked the Christophers immediately. They were a sophisticated couple who appeared to be in their early sixties. Nathan Christopher was a prominent black dentist, very mild-mannered and easygoing. I soon learned that one of his favorite pastimes was fishing in Canada. His wife, Edith, was the more outgoing of the two—a tall, authoritative woman who owned a couple of businesses and often fronted the capital to help young black business owners open their flower shops, beauty salons, and corner stores. She traveled in political circles and was not intimidated by powerful men or seemingly anyone. She was a big woman who wore bottle-thick glasses that only slightly improved her vision, which had been practically destroyed by cataracts. I helped drive her around, cook occasionally, and perform light chores. The couple had both a maid and a cook, so my chores didn't amount to much more than I already did at home.

This kind of arrangement was fairly common among black families who wanted to give back to the community—especially those who could comfortably offer college students free housing, food, and tuition assistance in exchange for their helping out around the house. I was the eleventh student the Christophers had welcomed into their home over the years. After raising their daughter and son into adulthood, the couple had committed their lives to nurturing the dreams of other black children, particularly those from families of lesser means. Their home was an elegant apartment on East Boulevard in an upper-middle-class, mostly white neighborhood, across from a nice park. I slept in a room that had been built as the "maid quarters," just off the kitchen in the back of the apartment. It was comfortable, though nothing fancy.

Because of where the Christophers lived, I was able to enroll in East High, an integrated but mostly white high school in the neighborhood. It was one of the best schools in the city, and fortunately for me, none of my peers knew my story. There, I was just another student trying to keep up with my schoolwork. It felt good to go to school without being noticed. The other students were friendly enough, but I didn't develop any lasting relationships, in part because my evenings were spent behind the wheel of Mrs. Christopher's navy-blue Lincoln, shuttling her from one meeting to another. But I rather enjoyed hanging out in the background of her life and watching quietly as this strong, smart black woman negotiated, gave orders, and made things happen. In some ways, she was the female version of my grandfathers, tough and re-sourceful. In her, I saw possibilities for myself.

Back then, I always liked spending time with older people like Mrs. Christopher because I believed they could teach me something. I sometimes learned by just watching how they handled themselves. I also enjoyed listening to their stories. Plus, I was very comfortable around them. But my time in Cleveland ran out sooner than I had expected. I had been living with the Christophers just one month when Mrs. Christopher called me into her room for a chat. She had never summoned me like this before, so I figured it must be serious. As I walked to her room, I quickly reviewed the past few days in my head, wondering if I might have done something she did not like. Nothing came to mind.

When I walked into the bedroom, Mrs. Christopher was sitting on the edge of her bed. She wore a smile that told me she wasn't upset with me, but the mood was less than happy. I took a seat in the chair across from her and braced myself as she began to speak. She and her husband really liked me, she said, but I wasn't exactly the kind of student she had requested.

I clearly wasn't deprived or lacking in social grace and skills, she said. I had been blessed with good, solid parents, grandparents, aunts, and uncles who were perfectly capable of providing whatever guidance I needed. She said she believed there were other students who might benefit more from her and her husband's help. She was very warm, almost apologetic.

I knew how important it was to her to feel that she was making a difference by providing an opportunity that a young person might not otherwise have. I didn't want to stand in the way of that. Mrs. Christopher had some other ideas for me, though. She didn't think I should return to Little Rock or Central. I was smart and mature enough to skip the rest of high school and start college as early as the coming summer, she said. She sat on the board of Ferris State College in Big Rapids, Michigan, and she assured me that I could get in.

I wasn't so sure. My gut told me that I wasn't quite ready for college. After an entire year out of school, I believed I needed more math and science to have a chance at success in college. But I told Mrs. Christopher that I would discuss it with my parents and think about it.

Mother and Daddy were flattered that a woman of Mrs. Christopher's stature thought I was ready for college, but they, too, had some concerns. We didn't rush into a decision. I applied to Ferris State, and we kept our options open.

During our frequent conversations and letters over the next few weeks, Mother and Daddy kept me abreast of the political changes taking place in Little Rock. A recall election in May resulted in a new school board, with a majority of moderates who proclaimed that Central would reopen in the fall. The votes of the city's black residents and affluent, well-educated white residents had made the difference, my parents said.

By mid-May, I received word that I had been accepted to Ferris State, but I decided not to go. My parents and I agreed that I should return to Little Rock to get my high school diploma because I needed to hone the academic skills required for college. But for me, there was an even greater need. I had been through too much over the past nearly two years—so had my family—for me to just walk away empty-handed. I needed my high school diploma, and I needed to earn it from Central. That accomplishment, I believed, was the least I could achieve now. Anything short of that would have felt like failure to me.

The problem was, even with the remote classes and my two months at East High, I was still short of the credits I would need to finish eleventh grade at Central. I needed to attend summer school. My parents arranged for me to spend the summer with relatives in Chicago and attend summer school there. In early June, I packed my bags, thanked the well-meaning Christophers for their generosity and kindness, and boarded a train bound for the Windy City.

Waiting for me there were my great-aunt M. E. Cullins Beard and her husband, Elmer. I called her Aunt M.E. She was the youngest sister of Grandpa Cullins (my maternal grandfather), and she reminded me so much of Mother. Aunt M.E. had no children of her own, but of all her nieces, she clearly favored Mother. She even called Mother her "pride and joy." Mother had picked up some of our aunt's ways, too, particularly her keen sense of fashion. Aunt M.E. was an avid reader of *Vogue* magazine and always looked as though she had stepped right off its pages. She wasn't just a fashion plate, though. She had attended Philander Smith College, taught school, and worked as a secretary. She had moved to Chicago from St. Louis after meeting and marrying Elmer Beard. They lived on the South Side, a typical Chicago suburb with neatly trimmed trees and well-kept lawns and hardworking professional and blue-collar families.

Many of the neighbors were former black southerners who had headed north, following kin who'd been part of the so-called Great Migration of the early twentieth century. They had come to break free of the stranglehold that Jim Crow had on the places of their birth. They had come in search of the opportunities touted by the *Chicago Defender,* one of the most widely read black newspapers throughout the South. They had come in search of jobs in Chicago's steel mills, meatpacking houses, and railroads, and the opportunity to learn, eat, and travel as freely as any white man or woman. They had come with nothing but their sheer will and ingenuity.

Here, up north, and generally during this time, I felt tremendous pressure to live up to everyone's expectations— my family members, Mrs. Bates, the NAACP. I wanted never to disappoint any of them. Most times, that wasn't difficult. My nature leaned toward following the rules and doing the right thing.

But that summer, I was a sixteen-year-old music

lover in a real music town with temptations along practically every street that I walked to and from school. I attended summer school at Hirsch High, about a mile from my aunt and uncle's home. My classes began at eight a.m. and ended at noon, just about the time that Seventy-Ninth Street began to sizzle. I mean, it was sizzling, literally, hot as heck outside. But the music scene was just as hot. In those days, the record stores blasted the latest music through huge speakers that filled the walkways with the soulful sounds of rhythm and blues, rock and roll, and jazz. Everywhere I walked, it seemed I heard Brook Benton's smooth baritone flowing through the speakers, heating up the already hot outdoors with his hit "It's Just a Matter of Time," which was topping the R&B charts that summer.

That's probably what first drew me into the record shop, but once I realized the place was air-conditioned, it gave me another excuse to stop by every day. I'd wander around the store, listening to the acrobatic voice of Jackie Wilson crooning "Lonely Teardrops." Fats Domino would start pleading in "I Want to Walk You Home," or jazz great Ahmad Jamal would take me to heaven gliding up and down the piano in his sensational "Poinciana"— I love that piece to this day. I'd linger in the record store, listening, losing track of time, sorting through the albums of some of my favorite artists: Little Richard, Elvis, and the original "queen of soul," Dinah Washington.

One day, while walking from school, I noticed a sign that Dinah would be appearing at a popular South Side club called the Roberts Show Lounge. I had to be there. It didn't matter that I was just sixteen or that I'd probably have to scheme to get inside. This felt like the chance of a lifetime. It helped that I had some cool, older family members whom I had gotten close to. One of them was Uncle Elmer's daughter from a prior marriage, Sue, who was a teacher, and her husband, George Love. Sue and George were lenient with me and helped to bridge the generational gap between me and their parents. When I saw the Dinah Washington sign, I knew I could rely on Sue and George to cover for me.

There was no cover charge at the door, and I just slid in with the crowd. I always acted older, and my height made me look older, too, so I didn't stand out. I didn't drink or draw attention to myself. I just sat in that grand lounge with the huge stage. A big crystal ball hanging in the middle of the room mesmerized me as much as the queen herself. As those crystals glittered and bounced off the ceiling, Dinah belted with ever so perfect timing and precision:

> *What a diff'rence a day makes*
> *Twenty-four little hours . . .*

Talk about glamour—Dinah took me there that night. It wasn't the last time Sue and George helped me witness what would become legendary Chicago music history. Later that summer when I saw billboards advertising a jazz festival, I gave Sue the $3.70 or so I'd saved, by walking instead of riding the bus to school, to buy my ticket. My parents were jazz lovers. Mother and Daddy would bring home the music of Duke Ellington, Billie Holiday, Sarah Vaughan, Pearl Bailey, Eartha Kitt, Earl "Fatha" Hines, all the popular jazz artists of the day. One of them was always playing in the background of our lives at home. So how was I supposed to resist when I saw on the billboard that practically all my favorite jazz artists would be playing at Chicago Stadium?

Again, Sue and George helped cover for me. They told me how to take the bus to the west side for what turned out to be one of the best days of my life. When I got to the stadium, I struck up a conversation with a police officer, who let me slip onto the floor for an unbelievable view. I could hardly believe my luck as I stood there, soaking up the best music I'd ever heard in my life: Count Basie, Joe Williams, and a group that I had seen the year before in New York, Lambert, Hendricks & Ross. The show was a real thrill. It made my summer.

As the summer wound down, my parents called me with big news. The federal courts ruled that the high school closings had been illegal. The high schools in Little Rock could now, finally, reopen. Suddenly, there was no more time to lose, and school officials were rushing to start the new school year early.

The opening of the 1959–1960 session—my senior year—was set to begin August 12, much earlier than the usual school opening after Labor Day. Unfortunately, summer school wouldn't end until the third week in August, and I would miss the grand reopening of Central.

It turned out that Gloria would remain in Kansas City to finish her senior year. By then, Minnie and Terrence had graduated from the high schools they had attended in other cities, Melba was preparing to take courses at San Francisco State University, and Elizabeth and Thelma had completed their senior year mostly through remote courses. Of the original Little Rock Nine, just two were left to return to Central: Jefferson and I.

I was surprised that even after two years of racist hostility over the integration, black students had still applied to go to white high schools when they reopened. Now a total of five black students would be going to Central: Sybil Jordan, Frank Henderson, Sandra Johnson, Jefferson, and I.

If anyone had any illusions that things would be different in the upcoming school year, those thoughts surely must have evaporated on the first day of school. I was finishing up summer school in Chicago on the morning of August 12 when back home in Little Rock, a caravan of segregationists from all over Arkansas descended on the State Capitol grounds to hear Governor Faubus make a speech. Family members told me how the governor fired up the crowd with his anti-integration rhetoric and how the streets filled afterward with an angry mob headed for Central.

But a new police chief was in charge—Chief Eugene G. Smith. I remembered Chief Smith from the 1957 school year. He was the one who had issued the order to get us out of Central on the day the mob took control. This time, Chief Smith had used a megaphone to order the crowd to disperse. The protesters paid him no mind.

When the crowd got more unruly, Chief Smith ordered firemen to open their hoses, unleashing a torrent of water streaming onto the crowd at half blast. For this, the segregationists would immediately come to hate Chief Smith and the fire department, and consider them among the number one enemies of their segregationist cause. (Years later, Eugene "Bull" Connor would apply that same controversial tactic on civil rights marchers of all races in Birmingham, Alabama, many of whom were children. Unlike Chief Smith, he ordered the hoses turned to full, not half, blast, powerful enough to strip bark from trees.)

About an hour after the mob quieted, Jeff walked up the steps of Central to begin his senior year. But he wasn't alone. Our comrade Elizabeth Eckford, who had finished her high school coursework remotely, knew I was still out of town and did not want Jeff to face the screaming, spitting segregationists on his own. She had known better than anyone else what it was like to stand alone in the middle of that hateful mob. Her decision was nothing short of brave and heroic. It touches me still.

Finally, summer school was over, and it was time for me to leave Chicago. Aunt M.E. and Uncle Elmer bought me an airline ticket so I could make it back to Little Rock in a hurry. I was excited to be headed home to see my family after five long months away.

But even more, I actually looked forward to returning to Central. There was something I needed to finish.

# CHAPTER 9

## First-Semester Senior

**W**hen I made it home from Chicago, a letter from the new superintendent of schools, Terrell E. Powell, awaited me:

> Welcome to Little Rock Public Schools for the
> 1959–60 school year. We are anticipating a
> fine year in every way. An identification card
> is enclosed for your use. Please sign it and
> have it with you at all times since you will be
> asked to present it for entrance to your high
> school.

School ID cards were practically unheard of in the 1950s South, as was the notion that anyone might try to enter a school with evil intent. But the segregationist mobs had forced school officials to change their way of thinking. On the morning of August 24, 1959, twelve days after school opened, I clutched my new ID card and headed to Central to start my senior year. When I arrived, I was surprised to find that the streets were quiet. The segregationists, who had returned to the sidewalks with their signs and chants for opening day, were long gone. I could feel the tension roll off my shoulders. I felt normal again, like just another student showing up for school.

As I climbed the front steps, the air was unusually quiet and peaceful. Even in the halls, my white peers seemed almost resigned to my presence. They weren't particularly friendly, but at least I wasn't harassed at every single turn. The long year off had left us all weary of the politics, I suppose. And we were just relieved to be back in school. Maybe, I hoped, we would find a way to coexist this year.

Like most Central students, I entered this school year feeling behind. I was nervous about taking algebra and Spanish after a long year away from those subjects. I also began chemistry with some trepidation because I had not taken Algebra II, which wasn't offered through correspondence classes. But the greatest source of my fear about chemistry was the teacher, whom I'd heard did not want any black students in his class. I'd learn soon enough that those fears were warranted. He was a young guy fresh out of college, and he tried hard to buddy with the roughnecks. I constantly had to watch my back in his class because the troublemakers felt comfortable enough with this teacher to pull their old tricks—glue in my chair, spitballs, flying ink. The teacher just turned the other way. I considered myself in survival mode and just lay low, kept my nose in the books, and kept my mouth shut. But Jefferson, who had the same teacher at a different time, struggled mightily with him. Jeff was a whiz in math and science, and when an answer or explanation didn't seem quite right to him, he questioned the teacher. The teacher seemed to bristle at even the notion that a black kid had the audacity to question him, and Jeff's grades suffered for it.

My other courses included speech, physical education, and English. Once again, I was the lone black student in all my classes. That made for some long and lonely days. While a few white acquaintances now felt comfortable enough to smile at me, exchange a few words in the halls or lockers, or partner with me in class, I missed having friends to share the school day. I missed the laughter and fun I remembered from my days at Dunbar. I missed feeling like a real part of my school. During my first year at Central, I had been so focused on survival that I hadn't spent much time thinking about all that I was missing. But this was my senior year, when I should have been looking forward to the milestones, like getting asked to the prom and taking photos with friends to immortalize those special days. Instead, I was just ready for the year to end.

My two best friends, Bunny and Peggy, were both away at school. I was accustomed to seeing Bunny only on holidays and in the summer because she had attended Palmer Memorial Institute, a college preparatory school in North Carolina, for all of high school. Most of all, I missed Peggy, who was in college at Arkansas State. When I first started at Central, Peggy had been the one who kept me up-to-date on what was going on with our black peers. I sometimes had attended school dances at Horace Mann with her. With Peggy gone, so was my main link to Mann and any semblance of a normal high school social life. Because black students still were not allowed to participate in extracurricular activities at Central, I had no student government events, basketball practices, football games, or pep rallies to attend after school. But I occasionally went out on dates with a guy who was a year or two older and attended Arkansas State. I think Mother and Daddy felt sorry for me, because they sometimes drove me to Arkansas State's football and basketball games. I'd go to the student lounge on campus called the Lion's Den, a popular hangout for the college kids, especially after the games. I had the most fun of my senior year in the Lion's Den.

Other community groups also offered support for

us five black students at Central by inviting us to their social events. One such group, a prominent community of Quakers, called American Friends, invited us to a play. But most days, I just went to school and spent the evenings doing homework. I even lost interest in talking on the telephone. The hateful prank calls still came with such regularity that the telephone had become associated with nothing but negativity, and I had little desire even to go near it. I didn't complain. It all would be over soon, I told myself. I just had to get through the next several months of school and graduate.

Most days, the five of us rode together to and from school. Our parents organized a car pool, with one of them or a relative picking us up at our homes each morning and dropping us off each afternoon. With the legal case behind us and the protests by segregationists more sporadic, there was little need for us to meet every day at the home of Mr. and Mrs. Bates. We students already knew one another, but we got to bond as friends during those short rides in the car and the lunch periods when two or three of us sat together.

Frank was a tall, big guy, built like an athlete, but he played no sports and was very studious. He had a gentle personality, was very friendly and well-mannered. Like Frank, Sybil Jordan was super studious. She was the brainy type who read voraciously, which gave her a maturity and worldliness beyond her years. She was deliberate in her speech and didn't use any of the slang of our day. In some ways, Sandra Johnson was her opposite, the effervescent one, always bubbly and upbeat. There was a naïveté about her; she seemed surprised by the mistreatment from our white peers. But she often found a way to laugh about it. Sandra was a distant cousin of mine, and our fathers were fellow contractors who traveled together to Los Angeles to find work when the segregationists tried to punish them by shutting them out of jobs.

Jefferson and I tried as best we could to help the three newcomers navigate Central, but I don't think there was any way to prepare them realistically for what they would face. The atmosphere inside the school had improved somewhat, or maybe we were just jaded. But the harassment continued. Some teachers reported the troublemakers—who then just did their dirty work less openly. Again, most of the students treated us as though we were invisible.

I'm sure that was as tough for the new black students as it was for me the first year. But after the drama of my sophomore year, just being left alone was good enough for me. Still, I knew better than to get too comfortable. I might enjoy a few peaceful days, and then out of the blue, something frightening would happen—a threatening note left in one of our lockers, name-calling in the halls, or an attack on one of the boys—to remind me that I was still unwelcome at Central. Then came Labor Day weekend.

I was sound asleep the night of September 7 when the red station wagon used by Fire Chief Gann Nalley exploded and burst into flames in the driveway of his home. Thirty-three minutes later, firefighters were still battling the blaze when a second explosion blew out the glass front of an office building eight miles away. The building housed Little Rock mayor Werner C. Knoop's construction firm. Then, five minutes after that, a third explosion and fire damaged the ground-floor administrative office of the school board. The blast was so powerful that it also blew out windows in a nearby monastery and shook fourteen nuns from their sleep. For forty minutes, the series of explosions and fires ripped through Little Rock and painted the dark night a fiery orange. Sirens and police cars wailed, crisscrossing downtown. As investigators combed through the smoke and ashes, they determined that arsonists had thrown fused sticks of dynamite into all three targets. All three buildings had been empty, thankfully, and no one was injured.

The "Labor Day bombings," as they were soon known, were all over the newspapers the next day and the weeks to come. Little Rock officials responded with anger and disgust. Their city was under attack, and someone would have to pay.

Police Chief Smith, a no-nonsense, law-and-order kind of guy, summoned all his men to work the case. Officers stood guard at the homes of city officials and school board members.

The bombers' three targets had something in common: They were people or organizations considered sympathetic to integration. So, who would have considered them an enemy?

The segregationists, of course.

Tips flowed into the police department. The nuns who had been awakened by the bombings in their convent near the school board office were able to provide a detailed description of the suspects' car. Two days later, Chief Smith arrested two men: E. A. Lauderdale, Sr., the forty-eight-year-old owner of a lumber and roofing supply company, who was known around town as the leader of the segregationist Capital Citizens' Council; and J. D. Sims, a thirty-five-year-old truck driver. Both men were charged with bombing a public building.

The next day brought the arrests and charges against three more men: John Taylor Coggins, a thirty-nine-year-old auto salesman; Jesse Raymond Perry, a twenty-four-year-old truck driver; and Samuel Graydon Beavers, a forty-nine-year-old carpenter who worked at the state mental hospital. Chief Smith announced that the bombers had planned a fourth attack of an office building. Heavy traffic downtown apparently scared the bombers away.

Sims quickly pleaded guilty for his role, after admitting to an *Arkansas Gazette* reporter that he had placed three sticks of dynamite under Nalley's car and thrown ten sticks into the school board office. He received a five-year sentence and agreed to testify against Perry and Lauderdale, the alleged mastermind. He was sentenced to three years in prison. Coggins and Perry also received three-year sentences. Beavers's trial was postponed for a year because of his poor health, but he was later convicted and received a similar sentence.

I turned seventeen the December after the bombings. I knew that by the time the bombers targeted city officials, they already had gone after Mr. and Mrs. Bates many times with burning crosses, rocks, bombs, and even bullets. Mrs. Bates had sent telegrams to the Justice Department and the White House, pleading for federal protection. Yet no one had stepped in to protect her. It seemed as if the authorities didn't care much when it came to a black family under attack. She and Mr. Bates ultimately relied on the security provided by dedicated neighbors and friends, who stood watch with their own shotguns and pistols outside the couple's home.

I have to admit that I paid little attention to the details of the Labor Day case at the time. I was just eager to put Central, the segregationists, the bombings, and all they represented behind me—so eager that I spent more time thinking about the future than the ugliness swirling around me. My graduation from Central was just months away, and all I could think about was where I would go to college.

Many of my friends at Mann were planning to attend historically black universities. While I've always had much respect for those great institutions, I wanted to explore all my options. I knew that I wanted to go to school out of state, and I began to research various colleges. Since no one at Central had reached out to me about college placement, Ernie's aunt, Mrs. Gravely, a counselor at Dunbar, was advising me. When Ernie came home for Christmas, he suggested I apply to Michigan State. I was lukewarm on the idea at first, but I trusted Ernie, who was now a sophomore there and a big fan of the school. So I applied. Several other colleges also caught my eye, including Brandeis in Massachusetts, Grinnell in Iowa, and the brand-new campus of University of California at Santa Barbara. I applied to all of them, too.

Mother relished the idea of having a daughter at an elite private all-girls school, so she pushed for Vassar or Wellesley. I just didn't think that kind of environment was for me. A coed school with people from all walks of life was more to my liking. Eventually, my heart settled in a big way on Antioch College in Yellow Springs, Ohio. The school had a work-study program that allowed students to take classes one quarter and work in their field of study for college credit the next. The program seemed so visionary. It would give me a chance to take classes in the medical field and explore whether I really wanted to become a doctor. Such real-world connections could also become a stepping-stone for future job opportunities. I was sold and couldn't wait to hear back. I still recall the moment I pulled the letter from the admissions office out of my mailbox and ran inside to open it. My heart thumped with such excitement and anticipation as I ripped open the envelope and scanned the letter for the answer I'd been waiting to hear. But just as quickly, all that excitement was reduced to a huge lump in my throat as I read that admissions officials were recommending I take a year off. The letter said the university was aware of the stressful years I'd endured at Central and thought that before settling into the seriousness of college study, I needed to rest. Then the letter said something like "We will hold a place for you for the 1961–62 school year."

I was devastated. Sure, I had gotten in, but I didn't want to wait another year. Leaving Little Rock to go to college was the one thing that had kept me motivated and hopeful. I felt that all my dreams were starting to slip away. I felt rejected. I folded the letter, put it away, and walked around for weeks in silent shock.

But life was about to get a whole lot worse.

# CHAPTER 10

## An Explosive Night

**W**hen I settled into my bedroom the night of February 9, 1960, it was raining mud. At least that's how it looked to me when I heard heavy wind and rain slapping against the house. I looked up at the window and saw thick droplets of rain mixed with red dirt sliding down the windowpanes.

It was about nine thirty, my favorite time of night. I savored those moments of solitude just before bedtime when I got to unwind, listen to the radio, and think. The house was quiet. Daddy hadn't come in yet from his nighttime job at Big Daddy's place. Loujuana and Tina, then eleven and four, were asleep in their room a few steps up the hall, and Mother was in her and Daddy's room near the front door.

I clicked on the clock radio resting on the nightstand. The AM dial was already tuned to one of my favorite stations, WLAC, which broadcast nightly from Nashville. It was one of a few white stations that brought the soulful sounds of black rock and roll, rhythm and blues, and jazz artists—the Platters, Little Richard, Fats Domino, and Etta James—to my white peers throughout the nation. It tickled me when I imagined that maybe some of my white classmates at Central were listening secretly, too. I particularly enjoyed a program called *Randy's Record Highlights,* which aired shortly after ten o'clock.

As I changed into my pajamas, my mind felt at ease. I'd made it to the home stretch at Central, I thought. For weeks, things had been calm, no protesters or major incidents, and graduation was fewer than four months away. I'd finally stopped sulking after the rejection from Antioch and decided on a college. My decision-making process had been quite simple: I accepted the first school that wrote to me with good news after the big letdown— Michigan State. Michigan State wanted me right then, and I was eager to be wanted. I had been in no mood to wait to hear from my second and third choices. By the time the acceptance letters came from Brandeis and the University of California, I had already settled on going to Michigan. I was even starting to get excited. I liked the idea of getting lost among the thousands of students on campus. I'd get to come and go as I pleased, and no one would even notice. Finally, I would have a normal life.

Dances. Concerts. Football games. Maybe even a boy-friend. I'd missed out on so much at Central.

I could hardly wait to end this chapter of my life and start anew. But for the moment, it was bedtime. I clicked off the light in my room, crawled into bed with my thoughts, and let Etta and Fats serenade me to sleep.

No sooner had I closed my eyes, it seemed, than I was shaken by a thunderous boom. The house shook. I could hear glass crashing to the floor in the front of the house. I shot up, my hands gripping the sides of my bed as if to steady the room. For a moment, I felt frozen in place. My eyes, wide with fear, darted around the pitch-black room. What *was* that? Was I dreaming? The explosion had come from the front.

Then, oh, my God—my little sisters! Mother! I had to find them. As soon as my bare feet landed on the cold floor, I took off running through my bedroom. My first stop was the den, just outside my bedroom door. It was eerily dark and still. I turned toward the hall and ran up to the front of the house.

Loujuana and Tina were standing in their nightgowns with Mother in her bedroom door. When I reached them, Mother and the girls looked dazed and bewildered but unhurt. We stared at one another, too shaken even to speak. Little Tina's eyes moved quickly from Mother to me, searching our faces for clues. A haze of smoke floated through the darkness. It seemed to be coming from the living room into the hallway, where we stood. The smoke hurt my eyes, and an unfamiliar scent filled the air.

It smelled as if something had blown up in a chemistry lab.

Inside, I was trembling. I felt helpless and horrified. And I needed Daddy. He would tell me everything would be okay and make me feel safe. But he hadn't yet made it home from his late-night shift. I suddenly felt a painful sense of responsibility, as though I needed to step up and somehow make the situation right. But I didn't know how. I could feel real panic rising in my throat. I had the odd thought that the usually serious, stoic Carlotta—the one who always felt her hard work and smarts would make everything okay, who had believed that anything was possible if she stood firm and stayed strong—was now at a total loss.

The sound of my mother's voice quelled my panic. She was calm and restrained, but I heard helplessness, too. "Call your daddy," she said.

Relieved to be doing something, I ran to the kitchen and dialed the numbers to Big Daddy's place as fast as my jittery fingers could move. Trying not to sound frantic, I asked for Daddy and told him to come home right away, that something bad had happened. He slammed down the phone and must have dashed right out. It didn't occur to me to call the police, but by the time I hung up the telephone, officers were knocking on our front door. Mother talked to them, and I stepped inside the living room with my sisters to take in the scene.

The blinds hung askew, partially ripped down by the blast. Mother had made nice white linen drapes and matching sheers for all the living room windows—the one overlooking the front yard and the two that sat on each side of a large fireplace. The drapes now looked dingy in the smoky room. They flapped wildly as the cold air and rain whipped through the newly shattered windows. Tiny shards of glass covered the floor. The sight made me unspeakably sad. Mother had worked so hard to get this room just right.

My gut was telling me that this was no accident. Someone had deliberately tried to tear my home apart. My eyes roved the room as if I were an investigator. Something had clearly exploded, but there wasn't a visible hole anywhere. Through the smoke, I could see that the rest of the room, thank God, had remained intact.

It didn't take long to connect the dots. Mr. and Mrs. Bates had had crosses burned in their yard and a brick thrown through their window. And the Labor Day bombings had destroyed both offices and homes of people connected to school integration. Could the segregationists have come after me in my home, just when it seemed my battle was almost over?

Two officers walked around the perimeter of our

house with flashlights. Mother closed the door again to wait for Daddy. Tina stepped toward Mother, unaware of the glass that lay between them. But Mother's sharp voice stopped her in her tracks.

"Get back," she said. "Put on some shoes."

The three of us girls rushed to our rooms and pulled on our shoes and bathrobes. By the time we made it back to the living room, Daddy was home. It had taken him less than ten minutes, but the waiting had felt like an eternity to me. The instant I saw him, I felt calmer. As I looked at him standing there in his black coat and matching hat, with his arm around Mother's waist, I knew he was about to take charge and get to the bottom of this. He was worried and wanted to know: Were we okay? He kneeled down to pick up Tina. Moments later, he disappeared outside with the police. Mr. Fox from across the street came inside to talk to Mother. I kept an eye on Tina and Loujuana, who wandered around the living room on their tiptoes, dodging the glass. Mr. Fox and Mother huddled nearby. My ears perked up. Mr. Fox tried to whisper, but I caught a word that sent a chill down my spine. I could hardly believe my ears: Did he just say "dynamite"? That was it. That was the strange smell.

Then I knew for sure: The segregationists had bombed my home. They'd resorted to dynamite to run me out of Central. They would stop at nothing, even murder, to keep me out. My knees felt weak as that terrifying reality sank in: My family and I could have been killed.

I suddenly needed fresh air. More than that, I felt compelled to see the damage for myself. At least then I'd know for sure what they had done. For me, knowing was a comfort. I could handle what I knew. It was not knowing that made me feel vulnerable and afraid.

Despite Daddy's instructions for us to stay inside, I felt pulled to the front door. I walked outside, and I was startled to see that practically everyone from the neighborhood had gathered out front in their nightclothes under umbrellas and plastic rain caps.

"Are you okay?" a voice yelled out.

I immediately regretted my decision to leave the house. I wanted nothing more than to disappear. Maybe it was naive to think that I could go outside and watch what was going on like anyone else, but that's what I wanted. To blend in. Even in that first year at Central, when the television cameras rolled constantly, I'd managed to stay mostly in the background and let Ernie, Melba, and Minnie do all the talking. Now I was the object of everyone's attention. And it horrified me to think that all my neighbors were standing out in the cold rain because of me.

I was chilled by yet another new reality: My decision to go to Central and to stay, no matter what, had brought violence, not only to my home but to my neighbors', to the people who'd watched out for me since I was a toddler. Any one of them could have been hurt by the explosion. My stomach churned with guilt and anger.

Still, I kept walking to the side of the house where the windows had blown out. Just a few steps later, I stopped dead in my tracks. There, at the base of the chimney, I could see where the dynamite had landed. A gaping hole, about two feet wide, showed just how powerful the blast had been. Bricks were strewn wildly about. All I could do was stand there, feeling myself becoming soaked with the heavy rain. What if the dynamite had gone through the window and landed in the living room instead of hitting the ground? Would my house still be standing? Would my family have survived? Would I?

Finally, I turned and walked slowly back through the door. I was numb—and that seemed to be how we all dealt with the shock. Mother sent Loujuana down the street to spend the night at Uncle Teet's house. Tina dozed on the sofa in the den. Mother and I stayed indoors, listening quietly to the loud banging from outdoors as Daddy and Mr. Fox boarded up the windows. First, we sat in the kitchen at the counter, each of us staring past the other into space. I felt more vulnerable than ever before. I wasn't normally the type that spent much time thinking about "what if," but I couldn't stop the thoughts flashing through my mind nonstop. My family and I were at the mercy of whoever had done this. Everything—our home, all the things that Mother and Daddy had worked so hard to attain, even our lives—could be taken away in a second with one more explosion. And maybe next time, it would be more "successful."

After a while, Mother went to check on Tina in the den, and I followed. Neither of us said a word for what seemed like hours. My heart was loaded with such guilt. What could I do or say that would either comfort or explain? Just breathing was all I could manage. As I looked at Tina lying there so peacefully, part of me yearned to trade places, to be too young and innocent to understand the hate that bred this kind of terror.

I snapped out of it when Mother turned to me and said that I should go back to bed. I could feel myself resist. How could she possibly expect me to fall asleep, as though this were any other night and our home had not just been attacked? But I knew better than to question her, so I did as I was told.

Back in bed, my brain was so crowded with thoughts that I felt dizzy. This was my house, the safest place in the world, until now. How could I possibly sleep? How could I ever feel completely safe again here? How could I ever feel safe again anywhere? It was one thing for the segregationists to spit and shake their fists at me at school, when I expected it. There, I still felt some control. I could refuse to let their words wound me. I could refuse to cry. I could remind myself what I'd been taught at home: that those who hate are just ignorant and that I must never, ever stoop to their level.

But it was an entirely different matter to be caught off guard in the middle of the night in the place where I'd known only love, peace, and protection.

I could feel myself harden with determination. These people didn't know me. I wouldn't quit. They couldn't make me. I'd come too far. They couldn't chase me away from my home, and I wouldn't run away from Central like a scared puppy.

Their plan had backfired: I felt more strongly than ever that I had as much right to be there as any white high school student who lived in the neighborhood. I *would* stay. I *would* graduate. And I *would* walk across that graduation stage. Or I would die trying. The clarity of that thought calmed me down, and I finally, somehow, drifted off to sleep.

The next morning, I got out of bed around six o'clock, like every other school morning, and quietly got dressed. Mother and Daddy were in the kitchen—who knows if they'd even been to sleep—when I walked in.

"Are you sure you want to do this?" Mother asked.

"Yes," I responded simply. "I'm sure."

Daddy knew me. He took one look at the determination in my face, and he knew there was no use trying to keep me at home. He shrugged as if to say, "If that's what she wants to do . . ."

It was exactly what I wanted to do, and I hoped my parents were proud of me for refusing to stay at home.

Before leaving for school, I went to see Tina, who was awake in the den. Standing in her nightgown in front of the television, she pointed excitedly at the screen.

"That's our house!" she exclaimed.

Sure enough, the bombing had made the national news, and images of our house were flashing across the television screen. Mother rushed in, scooped up Tina, and turned off the television.

From that day forward, my parents never said a word to me about the bombing. It was as if clicking the TV off could erase every memory of that horrible night. I knew that in my parents' minds, the bombing was grown-folks' business, not the kind of thing that should be on the mind of a child. As always, they believed they were protecting me from the side of life that I was not ready—or they were not ready for me—to handle. Soon enough, they figured, life would reveal its own ugly truths.

I didn't question their authority, so I didn't bring it up. By now, I had my ways of finding out things. I knew that, somehow, I would find out exactly what had happened and why.

While Mother drove me to school, I wondered if my white classmates and teachers had heard about the bombing. I wondered whether they even cared. I guess part of me yearned for some sign that at least some of them really did care.

But the not-so-subtle glares, whispers, and finger-pointing of the students milling around their lockers inside suddenly made me feel like an object of ridicule. Not one of them—not even the few acquaintances I'd made or the teachers who taught me every day—uttered a word to me the whole morning.

Weren't they even a little curious about the silent black girl sitting beside them in class, the one whose house had been bombed? Was it too much to expect a few kind words, a sympathetic smile, a friendly gesture? Even after all I'd been through at Central, I still expected at least that much. I had hoped that maybe some of them would think the bombing had taken matters too far, that they would think about my family and the tragedy that could have been. I had hoped that maybe now in my most vulnerable moment they would finally see *me,* Carlotta, the human being with a heart like theirs, a heart that was hurting.

Their silence affected me deeply. I felt more isolated than ever.

Back home that afternoon, Loujuana was back to her favorite games of making doll clothes and having her pretend tea parties. Tina was running around, as bubbly as any four-year-old. And Mother was back in the kitchen, busy as usual. I wasn't surprised. It was the family way: Don't look back or linger in pain. Pull yourself up. Dust yourself off. Straighten your shoulders. Lift up your head. And walk tall, no matter what.

Of course, no one ever said any of this out loud. No one had to. I'd seen it all my life in the way my parents, grandparents, aunts, and uncles had always lived. And now it was my turn to show that I'd learned their lessons well.

But I always wanted to know what was going on under the surface, beneath the silence. To stay informed, I had developed the art of listening and eavesdropping. I rarely missed a thing that was going on in my home. I also devoured the newspapers, particularly the *Arkansas Gazette*, the more progressive of the two local papers. Often, it was my only source of information. In the coming days, I saw my life unfold through the headlines.

The day after the bombing, the banner headline of the *Gazette* read: BLAST RIPS HOME OF NEGRO PUPIL AT CENTRAL HIGH. Two smaller headlines even mentioned me by name: CARLOTTA WALLS, FAMILY UNHURT BY EXPLOSION and CARLOTTA, ONE OF ORIGINAL 9 AT CENTRAL. Two days later, I read in the same paper that this was the first time in U.S. history that a student had been the target of a bombing.

The newspaper also reported that the force of the blast had broken windows in the house across the street.

Calls reporting the explosion had come from points more than two miles away. Neighbors told the paper they had seen two unfamiliar cars drive by the house just before and after the explosion—a crucial detail that seemed to go nowhere.

From all appearances, the police were trying to find the culprit. All the detectives in town were assigned to check out leads.

There was no question in my mind that the violence directed at me was linked to the Labor Day bombings. Some of the bombers were still out on bail. But if others had made the connection, they did not say so publicly. It was as if everyone were waiting for something else to happen.

I anxiously followed the developments in the newspapers. In the *Arkansas Democrat*, known as the pro-segregationist newspaper, local white leaders were speaking out—but not in defense of my family and me. Instead, W. F. Rector, president of the Little Rock Chamber of Commerce, was concerned that the turmoil had cost the city some big business prospects.

"This is a minor incident and we have been kicked in the teeth again," he stated.

Mrs. Bates fired back the next day in the *Gazette:* "It's too bad that Mr. Rector, who holds an important position in the community, would call a vicious, cowardly act of this kind a minor incident. People around the world are today judging American democracy by what is happening in Little Rock."

I appreciated Mrs. Bates even more every time I read a comment like that. Over the last three years, she'd stood in front of countless microphones, and when she opened her mouth, the fiery truth came out.

The most outrageous response to the bombing came from Amis Guthridge, chief attorney for the white Citizens' Council, an anti-integration group. In the newspaper, he suggested that "Negroes" might have been behind the bombing in some way.

The suggestion was insulting to our intelligence. It was so absurd that I couldn't even muster the energy to get angry. It didn't occur to me to be afraid.

I remained confident, though, that Police Chief Eugene Smith would be fair. It had taken him just three days to arrest the Labor Day bombing suspects. Yet the reward for finding the bombers then had been $20,000. This time, the reward was only $2,500, around one-tenth the amount. When I read this, I felt both infuriated and hurt.

I thought once more of how many times Mrs. Bates's home had been attacked. Yet no officials had protected or helped her. It seemed like the city's leaders just didn't care as much when the violence was targeted specifically at black folks. The limited reward to catch the bombers seemed to send a message that the bombing of our home was somehow less important. This despite the fact that, unlike the empty vehicle and buildings blown up during the Labor Day bombings, my home had living, breathing human beings inside.

My breakfast sat on the counter untouched that morning. And the door slammed a little harder when I left the house.

Thank God for the letters and telegrams that began arriving almost daily from around the world right after the bombing. They were, in part, what kept me going. Out-of-town family and long-lost friends sent heartwarming messages of encouragement. White strangers wrote touching letters. A few of the letters were written in a foreign language, and some even arrived with small amounts of cash or checks. But they all had one thing in common: They broke the silence. They let me know that this nightmare was not just mine and my family's alone, that people of goodwill from far away were watching and listening, that they were horrified by such evil, and that they cared.

Nine days after the bombing, as I'd feared, the other shoe dropped.

It was well after dark on February 18 when my father got home. He was still working nights at Big Daddy's pool hall to help make ends meet. The house was quiet except for my parents' voices coming from near the front door. I was in the kitchen, but my ears were alert for any news I could pick up.

"They want me to go downtown to the police station," Daddy said. I couldn't see him, but I heard the door open, then close behind him. I wondered: Where was Daddy going? And who were "they"? Nothing in his voice sounded alarming, so maybe the police had asked him to come downtown to answer more questions about the bombing. There was nothing to do but go to bed.

When I woke up for school the next morning, Daddy wasn't there. Mother was pacing back and forth in the kitchen. Her face looked more worried than I'd ever seen, so I knew right away that it wasn't simply that Daddy had left early for work. Mother tried to go about our morning routine, but I wasn't fooled. The front-page headlines helped to explain my mother's mood:

2 NEGROES HELD FOR WALLS BLAST.

POLICE GIVE NO MOTIVE FOR ACCUSED.

My eyes sped across the newspaper page and then froze when I saw a familiar name: Herbert Odell Monts. Police were accusing Herbert, my childhood playmate— the same Herbert who'd been a faithful player on our neighborhood softball team—of bombing my family's home?

Herbert was seventeen, just like me, and we'd been buddies practically our entire lives. We were born on the same day, just fifteen minutes apart, and grew up one block from each other. I could almost pitch a stone from my front yard to his. We had played softball and marbles, ridden our bikes, and walked the streets of our neighborhood together more times than I could count.

Another acquaintance, Maceo Antonio Binns, Jr., also had been accused. I could hardly believe what I was reading. This simply made no sense. Maceo, then thirty-one, was a regular at my grandfather's place, so my father knew him well. Maceo's sister and my family attended the same church, and I was friend with his nephew, McClain Birch.

Every day since the bombing had brought me to a new level of disbelief. Now I was in shock at the gall of the police to arrest these young men.

According to the newspaper, Herbert and Maceo had been brought in for questioning by local police and FBI agents five days after the bombing. At that point, despite the fact that witnesses had described strange cars on our street that night (just as they had after the Labor Day bombings), the cops had no leads in the case. Chief Smith announced the arrests at one fifteen that morning. He'd charged Herbert and Maceo under a statute that made it illegal to "willfully or maliciously destroy or injure property by means of an explosive," which carried a maximum penalty of up to five years in jail. It was the same felony charge that had been filed in the Labor Day bombings.

Once again, my breakfast went to waste. By the time I

finished the article, my stomach was in knots and I was full of questions. What in the world did these arrests mean? And what did they have to do with my father? He wouldn't have pointed the finger at Herbert or Maceo, who obviously had not bombed our home. Why was Daddy still away, and why hadn't we heard from him?

But as worried as I was, I told myself I could not overreact. With Daddy gone, I had to hold myself together for Mother and my little sisters. So I did what I always did on school mornings: got dressed and went to school.

I never even thought about not going. It was the only way I knew to fight back. Segregationists were behind all of it—the bombing and the arrests of Herbert and Maceo. If I stayed home even a day, those responsible might think they were winning. So my presence at school said to the enemy: You have not whipped me, whittled me down, or scared me enough to make me quit.

At times during the day, the anger and fear inside me felt like a fist in the pit of my stomach, but I refused to cry or even look afraid. I tried to appear nonchalant and intensely focused on my studies. An old report card from that time shows that I earned all As and Bs the first semester of my senior year. After the bombing, my grades tumbled to mostly Cs and a few Bs. My first C was made in tenth-grade Geometry, never to be repeated until my last six-week grading period after the bombing. So the events clearly took their toll, despite my determination.

The day at school felt surreal. Once again, none of my classmates or teachers said anything about the arrests. This time, I was so distracted that it hardly mattered. All I could think about was getting back home to see if my father had returned. What had the authorities done with him?

When I finally got home after school, Mother was still pacing. And Daddy still was not there. I knew now that the police cared nothing about black families when they carted off our loved ones. No one was going to contact us with an update. I flipped through the local telephone directory, found the number to police headquarters, and dialed it. Calmly, I identified myself and asked to speak to my father.

"He can't come to the phone," replied the voice on the other end.

"When is he coming home?" I asked, trying not to sound like a scared child.

There was no answer.

With each passing minute, the anxiety in our home rose like a quiet flood. Word about my father spread quickly, and relatives and friends from all over the country began calling. Every time the phone rang, my mother, sisters, and I all jumped.

Finally, Big Daddy came in with some news. He was well connected for a black man of that era, and he knew someone who had gotten "inside" information. FBI agents were involved, and they were asking my father lots of questions.

Of course, we worried that they were doing more than just asking questions. After all, this was the South, where a black man taken from his home in the middle of the night by whites—even the police, even the FBI—could face unthinkable horror.

As I lay in the darkness of my room that night, my mind zoomed in on Daddy. Was he okay? Were police hurting him? I shook the bad thoughts out of my head. Daddy *would* come home. He had to. Memories flooded my head: How he came home from work in the evenings and stopped outside to spend a few moments with me and my friends. How he'd turn the jump rope, pitch a few softballs to us, or find some other way to join in our fun. How I always slept better whenever he was in the house. He'd come in, bone-tired from working day and night, and I didn't even have to see his face to feel his presence. I'd hear the door open and close behind him, wait for the silent pause as he took off his straw hat, and then listen again for the light tap of his shoes across the hardwood floors that we had put down together. In those moments, my world suddenly felt safe again.

As the hours slowly ticked away on this long night, I couldn't close my eyes. I kept waiting for those sounds: his shoes, his voice, his laugh, something that said everything would be all right.

Instead, the next morning, I was greeted with the newspaper headline: POLICE QUIZ WALLS IN BOMBING: PROBE GOES ON IN SECRECY. In the distorted minds of white law enforcement officials, my father had something to do with the bombing! It was unfathomable to me that anyone could actually suspect that my father would be involved with attacking his own house while the love of his life and their three daughters slept inside.

Those next forty-eight hours dragged, and Mother and I seemed to sleepwalk through them. A haze of shock and fear hung over us as we tried to go about our daily routines. At least two days had passed since Daddy was taken away, and I still hadn't heard a word. Mother wasn't the type to cry in front of the children, but all of a sudden, I noticed that she began to take "a rest" during the day. She would disappear for maybe an hour behind the closed door of her bedroom and emerge looking somehow even wearier. My grandparents, aunts, uncles, and the Foxes were a constant presence in our house to keep us company. Of course, no one discussed Daddy's absence, but you could almost touch the tension.

Dusk was setting in one evening as I stepped onto the front porch for some fresh air. When I looked toward the street, the distant shadow of a tall man was walking slowly down the hill toward our home. His walk was unmistakable.

"Daddy!" I cried, dashing off the porch and down the road.

I threw my arms around him and held on tightly, wanting not to let him go ever again. My eyes scanned him up and down. He was wearing the same khaki pants he'd had on the night he left for work. His dark overcoat was slung across his arm. He was all in one piece, but something was wrong. Daddy wouldn't look at me. He kept staring straight ahead and didn't say a word.

I looked up at his face and found tears sliding down his cheeks. It was the first and last time I saw my father cry. What had he just been through? What had they done to him? Suddenly unable to speak, I just stood there. I felt as though I'd been submerged in ice water, cold and hardly able to breathe. My family was suffering profoundly because of me. And my determination to graduate from Central could have cost me my father. For the rest of the way home, Daddy and I walked side by side in silence.

Once again, I didn't dare ask questions. But, as always, I was paying attention and overheard things. Later, I heard Daddy telling Mother that for days the police had beaten him. They tried to force him to sign a confession, admitting that he and Maceo had planted the bomb to get the insurance money from the policy on the house. In the narrow minds of the police, Daddy was just a desperate Negro willing to blow up his own home and possibly even kill his family to get his hands on some money.

My heart raced and I could hardly breathe as I heard Daddy tell Mother how the police officers kept screaming at him:

"Do you know Maceo Binns?"

"Do you know Herbert Monts?"

Hours had turned into days as the officers kept taking him back and forth from a jail cell to an interrogation room. In his words, they were determined to make this figment of the FBI's imagination a reality—and they wouldn't give up. But they didn't know Cartelyou Walls. He wouldn't give up, either. And he refused to budge from the truth.

I stopped listening, went to my room, and wept quietly as I imagined Daddy's face, strong and determined, even while the officers beat him.

Within an hour of Daddy's arrival home, family, friends, and neighbors began stopping by to visit him. Daddy wasn't in the mood for company, so we politely turned them away at the door—all but Mrs. Bates. Daddy chatted with her awhile, and she insisted that he tell his story to Christopher Mercer, an attorney who was one of her advisers.

In the days afterward, Daddy's spirit seemed bruised. He was quiet and somber. And for what seemed like the longest time, we didn't hear his contagious laughter.

# CHAPTER 11

## Scapegoats

**M**y father was never charged in the bombing, but the ordeal was just beginning for Herbert and Maceo. A judge set a $15,000 bond for both of them.

"It sounds as if somebody's trying to railroad somebody," Mrs. Bates told the *Gazette*, in an interview about the weak, seemingly made-up case against Herbert and Monceo. "I can't understand why they would charge these two fellows. I don't know what evidence they have, but it sounds ridiculous to me."

Amis Guthridge, the white Citizens' Council attorney, seemed to gloat over news of the arrests. He was quoted at length, taking credit for getting Chief Smith to stop pursuing white segregationists as suspects and look inside the black community. And of course, Governor Faubus chimed in, saying that he had always questioned how such a thing could have benefited the segregationists.

The same day, the *Gazette* editorial praised the work of the police. The newspaper mentioned the absence of a motive but seemed to accept that the police had solved the case. In the same editorial, the newspaper declared that by all indications, "segregation extremists, like those convicted in the Labor Day explosions, had no hand in this case."

But the lack of a motive seemed to hang in the air. The next day, the *Gazette* again raised questions:

"Is that all of it, the two Negro suspects now in custody? If they did it, why?"

I never even pondered the questions because I knew that Herbert and Maceo had not bombed my family's home. Even though prosecutors had not charged my father, they didn't back down from their claim that he was the mastermind. In fact, the entire case against Herbert and Maceo seemed built on the notion that my father had recruited the two of them as part of a grand money-making scheme.

All I could do was hope that under the leadership of Chief Eugene Smith, who had always seemed fair and decent, the truth would come out somehow. I wondered if police had ever even investigated a neighbor's report of seeing unfamiliar cars in the neighborhood just before and after the bombing. It had been a detailed description of the getaway car in the Labor Day bombings that helped police track down those suspects. And yet Herbert and Maceo, who had zero evidence against them, were the ones sitting in jail. I felt helpless and guilty at the same time. Two innocent men could go to jail because of me, because I had been so determined to stay at Central.

Within a month of the arrests, things took another startling turn. I awakened one March morning to this shocking front-page headline:

**POLICE CHIEF KILLS WIFE, TAKES OWN LIFE AT HOME**

I gasped when I picked up the newspaper. I just could not believe that Chief Eugene Smith, then forty-seven years old, was capable of the kind of brutality described in the story. According to the newspaper, Chief Smith had shot his wife in the chest while both were seated at the kitchen table on March 18, 1960. As she fell backward, he shot her in the abdomen twice more. Then he shot himself in the left temple.

Mrs. Bates said that when she heard the news, she vomited and immediately had to be put to bed. She didn't believe the death of the couple was a murder-suicide. She suspected both had been murdered. Of course, no one will ever know for sure what happened in the Smith home that day. But to this day, I also believe it is likely that the police chief and his wife were murdered.

Chief Smith was loathed by white supremacists. They saw him as much too sympathetic to those of us involved in the integration of Central.

Now he was gone.

As crooked as the death of the Smiths and the arrests of Herbert and Maceo seemed, the mainstream media seemed satisfied that both cases had been solved. Any mention of the link between the bombing of my home and Central High School integration disappeared entirely from the headlines.

But Herbert's mother, Juanita Monts, wanted my family to know the truth about her son. One spring afternoon, she came to our door to speak to Mother. The two women stepped into our living room and sat on the sofa. I lingered in the hallway.

Mrs. Monts's voice sounded tired and sad. I felt tremendous sorrow for her. She had eight other children, six more boys and two girls, all younger than Herbert. I could only imagine how worried she must have been about her oldest child, who was in jail awaiting trial. Her husband, Hutella Monts, worked nights at Bell Telephone, and Mrs. Monts mostly stayed home with the children, though eventually she would return to college and become a full-time teacher. They were a close-knit, upstanding family.

Mrs. Monts spoke softly as she told Mother how terrible she felt about the bombing of our home. But she assured Mother that Herbert had nothing to do with it. It was important to her that we know that, she said. I've always thought that was such an honorable thing for her to do: to care enough about what my family thought of her son to tell Mother face-to-face that he was innocent.

"I know," Mother said softly.

We all knew. Herbert and Maceo were just convenient scapegoats of a system that seemed all too eager to protect the segregationists. I will never forget the image that day of the two mothers sitting there, both hurting, both bound by the fates of their two children.

About fifty spectators crowded into the courtroom for the first day of Herbert Mont's jury trial. To no one's surprise, the jurors who had been chosen were all white.

Prosecutor Frank Holt had bragged to the media that he had "a good case" against Herbert. In his opening statement, Prosecutor Holt said he would seek a maximum sentence of five years in the state penitentiary and a $500 fine.

Herbert, meanwhile, was represented by well-known civil rights attorney Harold Flowers. The white establishment in Little Rock already resented attorney Flowers for having defended and won cases for young black men in the past. This cast an even darker cloud over Herbert's trial before it got started.

Over two days, the prosecution called seven witnesses, mostly detectives and FBI agents, who reported that Herbert had "confessed." I knew that the same law enforcement authorities had beaten my father and tried to force him to confess to whatever they fed him. But Daddy was a grown man, a military war veteran who had seen the world and wouldn't be broken by white law enforcement authorities. Herbert was just seventeen. He must have felt frightened and alone, unsure of what to do to stop the madness. What choice would he have had but to sign whatever they were forcing him to, just so they would stop brutalizing him?

The prosecutor concocted this version of events: Herbert tried to light a match to light the dynamite, but the head of the match broke off. Then Maceo lit the fuse while Herbert ran home, drank a cup of coffee, and went to bed. Officers testified that Herbert told them that when he heard the explosion, he got dressed again and went out to see the damage.

I shook my head in disbelief at the lies being presented as truth in a court of law. What they were suggesting didn't add up. The prosecution even tried to use Herbert's intelligence against him by calling his science teacher to the stand to testify that Herbert was a good student, smart enough to build a homemade bomb.

My mother was called to the stand. Mother testified that she had been in bed about forty-five minutes and was asleep when the explosion occurred. When she was asked about the Monts family, she replied: "We're good neighbors."

Mother also testified that the money from the insurance company was a tiny amount, barely enough to cover the cost of the repairs from the bomb. There was no upside to bombing our own house.

Before resting his case, Prosecutor Holt also called Marion Davis, who said he had been hanging out with Herbert at my grandfather's place and that the two of them had left, walking home together. Marion testified that they reached his home first and that Herbert continued walking alone. Then Prosecutor Holt delivered what I'm sure he considered his "smoking gun." One of our neighbors, Earzie Cunningham, whom I did not know, testified that he had seen Herbert running from the direction of my home at the time of the bombing.

When it was Herbert's lawyer's turn to put on a defense, he called a single witness, our neighbor Reverend O. W. Gibson, pastor of our family's church, White Memorial Methodist. Reverend Gibson testified that he visited Monts in jail February 19 and noticed that one side of his face was swollen.

But Holt, on the prosecutor's side, called a rebuttal witness: an FBI agent. The agent testified that Reverend Gibson had filed an official complaint on March 2, saying that Herbert had told him he had been kneed and struck across the face by officers who interrogated him. The FBI agent, of course, denied that Herbert had been beaten.

Attorney Flowers did not call a single witness to challenge the timing of the prosecutor's account—how long it might have taken, for example, for Herbert to run up the block from my home to his house, drink a cup of coffee, and get into bed. Nor did he challenge whether it was even possible for all of this to occur while a fuse was burning down. He called no one to point out the glaring lack of fingerprints or any other physical evidence linking Herbert to the crime. Most important, he did not challenge the prosecution's sole "evidence"—Herbert's alleged confession. We would learn later when Maceo went to trial that such a challenge might have made all the difference for Herbert.

The white jurors took just thirty-eight minutes to deliver their verdict: Guilty.

Herbert was sentenced to the maximum five years in prison.

The outcome did not surprise me. By then, I'd lost all hope that justice would prevail. But I hurt deeply for Herbert, his family, his compromised future, his deferred dreams. There was nothing I could do to help, and thinking about him hurt too much. So I pushed Herbert's case to the back corners of my mind and heart, along with all the other injustices I'd endured and witnessed in Little Rock. It was the only way I knew to survive.

Nearly fifty years would pass before I would allow myself to go back to all that hurt. Then I'd learn the full story of how my friend had landed in the hands of the Little Rock police and what really happened to him.

But on that day in May 1960, as the judge pronounced Herbert's jail sentence, I could see only as far as my graduation from Central. It was just two weeks away, and all I wanted was to get that diploma in my hand and get out of Little Rock—for good.

# CHAPTER 12

## Graduation and Goodbye

**W**hen spring rolled around, the last thing on my mind was the prom. I heard the white girls in my classes excitedly discussing their dresses and dates. I still wasn't allowed to participate in extracurricular activities at school, so attending the prom at Central was not even an option. By then, I didn't have an ounce of energy to worry about it. I was tired. Plus, the bombing had altered my perspective about the things in life that really mattered. The prom just wasn't important. I was counting down to graduation and getting out of Little Rock, and anything else seemed like a distraction.

My parents saw things differently, though. What they saw made them sad. They saw a daughter who someday would have nothing but horrid high school memories, a daughter who would have missed out on some milestones of growing up. They set out to change what little they could. They got me an elegant class ring in yellow gold, with the school's name encircling a mother-of-pearl center. Then Mother and Daddy started dropping hints about the prom at Horace Mann. I should find out when it would be held, they hinted. I could invite that nice college boy who had taken me out a few times. They even promised to buy me a new dress.

I agreed. True to her word, Mother took me shopping at some of our favorite stores, and we found a cute baby-blue nylon gown with layers of lace from the waist to the floor. Underneath, I wore a crinoline slip with lots of netting that gave my dress the traditional southern belle flair. Arthur "Nick" Winstead, the college guy, was my date. He picked me up, and we spent a few hours at the prom, dancing and mingling with some of my old friends. It was a nice evening, and I'm glad I had the experience. But I can't say I truly felt like a part of the festivities. While I knew many of the students there through the community and through my old elementary school, I didn't go to school with them anymore or feel quite as connected. Afterward, I went back to sleepwalking through the days and counting down the time left at Central.

As graduation drew nearer, school officials gave each graduate six tickets for family members to attend. I was excited just to hold the tickets. They were a tangible sign that this was really happening. I would graduate from Central High School.

But as excited as I was, I couldn't shake the uneasiness. The attack on my home had left me feeling vulnerable. I knew in my heart the real bomber was still out there, and I couldn't help wondering whether my graduation might provide the perfect opportunity to strike again. The segregationists had been suspiciously quiet all spring, but I knew better than to think they had just accepted defeat.

My anticipation of graduation only heightened when I began receiving cards and letters of congratulations from extended family, friends, and even strangers. On May 24, this kind note arrived from my maternal grandmother, Erma, who still lived in St. Louis:

"I am so glad for you to get it over with. I hope you will not have to go through with this anymore during your school times."

I also heard from Grace Lorch, the compassionate white woman who had helped get Elizabeth safely to the bus on that first day when she had been separated from the rest of us and was surrounded by the white mob. Mrs. Lorch and her husband, Lee, had been branded Communists and harassed mercilessly over the years for sympathizing with us. I hadn't heard from or seen them in a long while.

"Very exciting news is coming from all over the South these days," Mrs. Lorch wrote, "but you and the other children in Little Rock were pioneers."

Many of those who wrote called me a trailblazer and

thanked me for my courage. Their letters reminded me of how much strength I had drawn from them over the years, those distant friends and family, as well as strangers, who took the time to let me know that they were with me in spirit—even when it felt like all of white Little Rock stood against my comrades and me.

The last days of May rolled by, and finally, it was May 30, 1960. Mother, Daddy, Loujuana, Tina, Big Daddy, and my mother's aunt Henrietta—Grandpa Cullins's oldest sister, and the matriarch of the Cullins family— joined the crowd in Quigley Stadium that Monday night. When Jefferson and I marched into the packed stadium with the 423 graduates in the Class of 1960, there wasn't even a chance that I would spot my six relatives in the crowd. But just knowing they were there filled me with pride. I wanted to walk tall for them. As I sat through the ceremony, I thought about those tough early days at Central—the sneering white mobs, the hallway battles, the exhausting days and sleepless nights. I thought about the bombing, Herbert and Maceo, and I wondered what would become of them. I thought about Michigan State. How eager I was for a fresh start, to leave behind Little Rock and every sorrowful memory I had accumulated there.

I snapped out of my daze when I heard Jefferson's name and watched him take his dignified walk across the stage. We had been true comrades from the beginning, and here we were together at the end of this leg of our journey. I was proud of him. And then . . .

*Carlotta Walls . . .*

Relief washed over me like a cooling rain when I heard my name. It was all over: the isolation, the harassment, the death threats, the terror. I'd come a mighty long way to get to this day. I pushed back my shoulders and held my head high as I walked across the stage, just as Ernie had two years earlier. I thought about my comrades— Melba, Minnie, Terry, Gloria, Elizabeth, and Thelma— who had started this journey with me three years earlier but never got to take this victorious walk. I was walking for them, too. We had risked it all and made it through.

I thought about Rosa Parks, that gracious woman whose courage I had tried to emulate on my toughest days at Central. I thought about Emmett Till, the teen-ager whose battered body had shown me the raw evil of the Jim Crow South. I was no longer the naive fourteen-year-old girl who had been shocked by the hatred and fear of my white classmates and their parents. Central had forced me to grow up, to learn some painful lessons about courage, perseverance, and justice. I was ready for whatever lay ahead.

The stadium was quiet as I accepted the diploma and shook Principal Matthews's hand. Just like Ernie's, who had crossed the same stage two years ago, my name was met with silence. I imagined my family cheering, though, the way they had done so many times in my life. I must have floated to my seat.

Afterward, I found Mother and Daddy and the rest of my group, and they all greeted me with hugs. The other graduates and their families seemed too excited even to notice me, and for a final, brief moment, things felt normal. Soon enough I handed over my robe and mortarboard, accepted my report card and diploma, and with that, my days at Central High School came to an end.

Later that night, Jefferson and I—the two remaining Little Rock Nine—celebrated together with our friends and families. A graduation party was held in our honor at a hall on Ninth Street. I couldn't remember the last time I'd felt so free. We danced all night long to the rock and roll and R&B sounds that over the years had added soul to our suffering. A new Jackie Wilson song was a big hit with the crowd that night. The lyrics were sung to a woman, but they also struck me as a kind of farewell ode to Central High:

> *You better stop, yeah, doggin' me around.*
> *If you don't stop, yeah, I'm gonna put you down . . .*

For all the celebration, Jefferson and I still had one more thing to complete before we were truly done with Central High School. The previous year of correspondence courses and summer school had left both of us short one unit required to graduate. The closing of the high schools in the 1958–1959 school year had cost us all so much. But school officials had decided to let us participate in the graduation ceremony and make up the missing unit over the summer. Elizabeth and Thelma, who had finished all their other required courses, needed to make up a single unit, too. All of us arranged to attend Beaumont High School in St. Louis, Missouri.

The morning after my graduation, my parents and sisters drove me to the train station downtown, and I took the first train out of Little Rock. There were no long, sad goodbyes. I hugged my sisters and parents, who reminded me that they would see me at the end of summer. I had been anticipating this moment all year. As my train rolled out of Little Rock, I knew that was the end of my time there. I'd never return to live. I had little desire to return even for a visit. My mind was fastened on the future. There was no time for looking back.

I was bound for St. Louis, where Elizabeth, Thelma, and I stayed with Frankie Muse Freeman, a civil rights attorney who served as legal counsel to the NAACP. Ms. Freeman was a dynamic woman who, like Mrs. Bates, was treading in deep waters that had been the sole domain of men. I loved her, and was excited for the opportunity again to live with and be influenced by a strong, professional black woman.

While I was in St. Louis, Maceo Binns's trial for "bomb-ing our home" began. I followed the case in the black press.

An all-white jury was selected. All three black resi-dents in the jury pool were dismissed.

Prosecutor Frank Holt, the same lawyer who had argued the case against Herbert, called ten witnesses be-fore resting his case. Mother was called to testify and was questioned about my father's absence from our home at the time of the bombing. As was the case in Herbert's trial, our neighbor Earzie Cunningham testified about seeing Maceo in the neighborhood near my house at the time of the bombing. Marion Davis, Herbert's friend, tes-tified that Maceo had been with him at my grandfather's café and pool hall that night. The same detectives who testified at Herbert's trial were called to answer ques-tions about the confession Maceo had signed.

Maceo was represented by attorney Will W. Shepherd, who, thankfully, was much more aggressive than Herbert Monts's lawyer had been. He actively cross-examined the detectives. According to media reports, Shepherd asked if they used "pressure as hypnosis" to get Maceo to talk. One detective admitted that "psychology" was used but refused to call it "coercion."

Maceo finally took the stand and angrily denounced the confession. He said he signed it because he'd been at his wits' end. After two days of nonstop questioning, authorities still wouldn't permit him to take a bath, talk to a lawyer, or even call his family. It had been torture. He said detectives told him that he would be released only if he signed the confession and that he could just deny it later. Maceo also reported that one detective even threatened to use a hose on him.

Maceo grew flustered on the stand. When Maceo's temper flashed in frustration, Prosecutor Holt asked: "Why are you getting mad?"

Maceo shot back: "Because you're trying to say I was someplace where I wasn't."

Maceo didn't stop there. He pointed his finger at Holt and exclaimed: "I don't know who did it. . . . As far as I know, you could have done it, and I'm not being facetious."

Prosecutor Holt called ten witnesses before resting his case. My father was called to testify for the defense, to say that all claims against him were untrue. Maceo admitted to passing my house in his car the night of the bombing. He said he was on his way to the medical center to pick up a girlfriend and that he passed Herbert, who was on his way home from the pool hall. Additional witnesses backed up Maceo's claim that he was parked at the medical center, waiting for a girlfriend, at the time the bomb exploded.

Nevertheless, the all-white jury, made up of eleven men and one woman, took just thirty minutes to find

Maceo guilty. Like Herbert, Maceo was sentenced to the maximum five years in prison. However, Maceo remained free on bond while his case worked its way up to the state supreme court. Nine months later, the state's high court would overturn Maceo's conviction in a 6–1 ruling that said confessions obtained after a fifty-seven-hour period of interrogation could not be introduced.

A new jury trial was set for Maceo to be held on December 7, 1961, but there is no record that the trial was ever held. As far as I know, Maceo was never retried and did not go to prison. I never saw him again after I left Little Rock. Cemetery records show that he died on January 13, 1972. He was just forty-two years old.

After Maceo's conviction was overturned, Governor Faubus commuted the sentences of three of the Labor Day bombers: J. D. Sims, John Coggins, and Jess Perry. Then, two months later, he reduced the sentence of the only Labor Day bomber still in jail, E. A. Lauderdale, Sr., making him immediately eligible for parole. After all those young black men had been through, the people who had likely actually been the bombers were getting out early.

By then, though, my parents had already cut their ties to Little Rock.

At the end of my summer at Beaumont High School in St. Louis, Mother and Daddy drove to pick me up, and we traveled together to East Lansing. They stayed a couple of days to help me get settled on campus at Michigan State. During those long hours on the road and in my dormitory room, Mother and Daddy gave no indication that they were contemplating a major life change. But about two weeks after they left me in Michigan, I received a shocking letter. The first thing I noticed was that the letter listed a return address in Kansas City, Missouri. Their letter said simply that they had moved there with my sisters. That was it. There wasn't a word of explanation, nor were there any expressions of sentiment or regret.

My parents never explained how long they had been contemplating the move or why they left when they did. Little Rock was all both of them had ever known. Except for my father's tour of duty during World War II, neither of them had ever lived more than ten minutes from their family and friends. The final decision to venture beyond that safety net must have been gut-wrenching.

Their sudden move told me what they could not: that I wasn't the only one who yearned for a fresh start.

# CHAPTER 13

## Finding Focus

At Michigan State, I was happy to be just a number. More than twenty-four thousand students attended the East Lansing university, and nearly one thousand of us were black. My schoolmates barely even noticed when I walked past. After three years of being at the center of so much negative attention, I was grateful for the chance to blend in with the crowd.

The university was like a city unto itself, spread over fifty-two hundred acres. It drew students of all races from every part of the country and the world. Being around people with such diverse backgrounds was exciting to me, and I made friends easily. Few of them realized at first that I was one of the nine black students who had gone to Central High School in Little Rock. I certainly didn't volunteer any information. But when they learned I was from Little Rock and saw me hanging out with Ernie, they began asking questions. They didn't bombard me, though, and gave me the space I needed from Central. I had left my past in Little Rock.

For the first time, I had true social freedom. I could come and go as I pleased, without anyone watching over me and without fearing for my life. And there was always plenty to do. One of my frequent hangouts was the student lounge. On weekends, I often joined my new friends at the fraternity parties on campus. And then there was football.

Football has always been at the center of social life at Michigan State. It quickly became the center of my social life, too. In Little Rock, I hadn't been allowed to go to Central's games, so I rooted for the teams from Dunbar and Horace Mann. Michigan State had one of the top football teams in the Big Ten Conference and was usually a championship contender. The atmosphere was always electric.

My knowledge of sports helped me to befriend many of the players, including Herb Adderley, a star offensive back who was the first black tri-captain for the Spartans. He was dating my roommate and was drafted in 1961 by the Green Bay Packers. I also became great friends with basketball standout Horace Walker, who had been drafted by the St. Louis Hawks. Horace was doing postgraduate work at the university, and I met him at a gathering for black students at an apartment in Lansing. He would become my best friend, the big brother I never had, and the godfather of my children.

At Michigan State, I was experiencing the exciting college life I had envisioned, except one thing. For the first time in my life, I was struggling academically.

I had known since I was a little girl what I wanted to do with my life. I'd even chosen Central in part because I believed it would better prepare me for that career path. So I decided right away to declare a major in premed. But after reviewing my transcript, the freshman counselor wasn't sure I was up to the task. I was missing some high-level math and science courses that I had not been able to take via correspondence or summer school in my junior year when Faubus shut down Little Rock's high schools.

"I can put you in the premed program, but you're going to have trouble," the counselor told me.

That comment sparked the part of me that couldn't stand people telling me what I could not do. I took the counselor's doubt as a challenge and insisted on being placed in the program anyway. I didn't recognize then that I was mentally exhausted. I just wasn't ready to work as hard as I would need to work to catch up academically. I was ready to have some fun.

The question in my mind about whether I could make it in premed grew bigger. I wasn't accustomed to making bad grades, and I was very frustrated with myself. My roommates—Ann Wynder, Connie Williams, and Ina Smith—encouraged me to study harder and seek help from a student counseling center on campus. I went to the center a couple of times but didn't find it very effective. I had some thinking to do during the quarter break.

That Christmas, I joined my family in Kansas City for the holidays. I found that my parents and sisters had settled in a wonderful, family-oriented neighborhood on Mersington Street. They had grown close to some of the neighbors, who had children the same age as my sisters. Mother was working part-time, since those icy midwestern winters often left Daddy out of work. It was good to see them so relaxed and happy. I couldn't bring myself to tell them I was struggling in school.

I returned to Michigan State for the winter and spring quarters, but I continued to have trouble as my core courses got tougher. Summer break gave me the time away that I desperately needed. I took the train to New York to spend the summer there, working for the Hotel Employees Union #6, the group that had sponsored the New York trip for the Little Rock Nine in the summer of 1958.

Now on my own, I wanted to immerse myself in the Sugar Hill neighborhood I'd heard Mother rave about during my childhood. I wanted to touch and feel the Harlem I'd read about in stories hailing the 1920s renaissance. I wanted to set my feet in the legendary jazz clubs, like

Smalls Paradise, which along with Harlem's Cotton Club was one of the popular nightclubs and restaurants in the 1930s and 1940s. It was Smalls Paradise where I first saw the husband-wife jazz duo Shirley Scott (on the organ) and Stanley Turrentine (on saxophone). I also spent time in Midtown on West Fifty-Second Street, listening to and watching the antics of Thelonious Monk.

Harlem never slept. When I stepped into a high-rise apartment for an after-hours party at two o'clock one morning, I got a taste of what I'd imagined Harlem was like during its great renaissance. Several artists lived there. My friends pointed out the apartment of one of my all-time favorites, Count Basie, and I lingered in the halls to be close to the sights, sounds, and smells all around. The intoxicating scent of food saturated the halls. The melodies of horns and a piano wafted out from one apartment, and the strong, bluesy vocals of a woman singing rang out from another.

New York was also home that summer to Ernie and Terry, who were working for the summer in the garment district. We were all hoping to save money for college. Ernie helped arrange for me to rent a reasonable room from the mother of a friend of his, who lived in Jamaica, Queens. The low cost of the rent helped me save enough money to buy a heavier winter coat and thicker sweaters than the ones I owned and to return to Michigan State with a few extra dollars.

Before heading back to Michigan State, I took a detour to Denver to visit my uncle Byron Johnson and his family. Uncle Byron was a distant relative on the Cullins side, but our family tradition was to call all family elders "Uncle" or "Aunt," no matter the relation. He was always one of my favorite family members. He was one of the kindest, most easygoing men I've ever known.

During my first year at Central, Uncle Byron had helped me with biology projects and offered constant encouragement. The next year, he and his wife, Christine, who had been childhood sweethearts, relocated to Denver with his job at the U.S. Postal Service. They had invited me to spend a few days during my first summer break from college with them and their two children—Jackie, who was fourteen, and their son, Joseph Byron, then seven.

The first thing I noticed and loved about Denver was its cleanliness. The entire city just seemed to glisten, and the air was fresh. My mind seemed at ease when I spent a few moments gazing at the white-capped mountains. People were polite, and the color of my skin seemed not to matter.

I spent less than a week in Denver, but the city stayed on my mind. I think Uncle Byron and Aunt Christine could tell that I didn't seem happy because they made what seemed to me a generous and tempting offer: If things didn't work out for me in Michigan, I was welcome to move to Denver with them, to work and go to school there.

When I returned to Michigan State for the fall quarter, I couldn't get Denver out of my head. I was disappointed in how my post-Central life was progressing. I continued to struggle in math and science and realized that maybe the counselor had been right: I wasn't prepared for the tough, premed curriculum. The lost year at Central had hurt in lasting ways. Not only had I missed out on essential coursework, I was having trouble focusing mentally on my studies. I just couldn't find the motivation. This was unfamiliar territory for someone who always had been a stellar student.

Maybe the admissions office at Antioch College had been right when they suggested I take time off before college. Though that advice had been so disappointing at the time, perhaps I should have listened. But it was too late for second-guessing. I was tired of struggling and in need of some serious self-care. Finally, I decided to let go of the medical field and just focus on taking my core courses.

My life seemed at a serious crossroads.

Sometime during my sophomore year, Aunt Christine sent me a ski sweater—a soft green cardigan with a black-and-white strip that zipped in the front. It reminded me of Denver, the mountains, and fresh air. I could enjoy skiing, I thought. I stuck it out another quarter at Michigan

State and stayed through the summer to take a few more courses and work. Mother and Daddy thought I was working at the telephone company, but I was actually a server at a little place called Sonny's Lounge. It was a fun job that gave me free access to good music and interesting people.

At the end of summer, I packed everything I'd brought with me to Michigan State and got on the train headed back to Kansas City. The weeks there passed quickly. As September rolled around, Daddy grew suspicious. He noticed that I had said nothing about returning to Michigan State and had never unpacked my trunk.

"When are you leaving to go back to Michigan?" he asked.

I hadn't figured out how to bring it up before now.

"I'm not going back," I told him.

Daddy remained cool. "Well, what are you planning to do?" he shot back.

I knew I had to have a plan. After high school, girls were expected to get married, go to college, or go to work. I'd left a scholarship behind at Michigan State. So I knew my plan had better be convincing.

"I'm going to Colorado," I responded. "Uncle Byron and Aunt Christine said that I could come to Denver, stay with them, work, and go to school if I want to. That's what I want to do."

My parents were always pretty good about letting me

make my own decisions. This time was no different. They asked a few questions, but in the end, they agreed to let me find my own way. Afterward, I called Uncle Byron and Aunt Christine to make certain the offer was still good.

"Sure," Uncle Byron said. "Come on."

In mid-September 1962, I boarded a Greyhound bus with my loaded trunk, bound for Denver and, I hoped, a fresh start. The trip took about eighteen hours—so long that I was able to finish reading a six-hundred-plus-page novel.

Once I arrived in Denver, I applied for a job with Mountain Bell, the local telephone company. I was offered a position as a service representative. But when I found out that I would be the very first black employee in my new job, I got worried. I couldn't go through that again. I didn't want to be the center of attention, a racial symbol, or the standard-bearer of anyone's expectations. I declined the position and asked to be a cashier/teller instead.

I had been on the job for nearly two months when my parents and sisters came to Denver for Thanksgiving. Uncle Byron immediately began trying to woo Daddy to the city for good.

"So, what do you think?" Uncle Byron asked after showing Daddy around.

"I figured I'd be hip-deep in snow and couldn't work," Daddy responded.

But Daddy was surprised to learn that the winters in Denver were more agreeable to construction work than the icy winter months in Kansas City. He agreed to come to Denver in January for work. The two of us shared the basement at Uncle Byron and Aunt Christine's home. Daddy transferred his union membership, found work right away, and was surprised to run into other brick masons from Little Rock. Soon he was hooked on Denver, too.

By the time Daddy arrived, I had enrolled in night courses at the University of Colorado for the winter/spring semester in 1963. I worked all day as a teller at the telephone company and then walked the two and a half blocks to class. But during the two-hour break between work and school, I often stopped at a lounge to listen to jazz, a beauty college to get my hair cut, or anywhere along the way to avoid arriving on campus early. I still wasn't quite focused on college.

When Mother and my sisters made it to Denver, my parents rented half of a duplex for a couple of months until they found a house they wanted to buy in the Park Hill neighborhood. We all moved into the new house together.

Park Hill had been an all-white, upper-middle-class neighborhood, but many white residents were beginning to move out as black families relocated there. One day,

Mother answered a knock at the door and found Reverend J. Carlton Babbs, pastor of Park Hill United Methodist Church, standing there. He told Mother that he had heard we were new to the neighborhood, and he invited us to worship with his congregation. My parents thought it was such a gracious gesture that all of us attended services the following Sunday. When we got there, we saw only white families. We learned later that just one black family was among the three-thousand-member congregation and that Dr. Babbs was reaching out to the new neighbors in an effort to integrate his congregation. The members were friendly and welcoming, and my sisters made friends at church youth programs. Park Hill was a good match for us all. My family soon became members, and we still worship there today.

Soon after we joined the church, a couple of my friends mentioned that they were preparing to go to DC for the March on Washington for Jobs and Freedom, a massive civil rights rally organized by civil rights leaders. I had no intention of going. I just didn't feel compelled to be part of the crowd. All of us have different roles, different ways of contributing to the common good. While I had tremendous respect for the leaders who organized the event, I had no burning desire to participate after all I'd been through.

But I must say that when I clicked on the television on

August 28, 1963, I was moved by what I saw—hundreds of thousands of men, women, and children of every hue stretched from the Washington Monument to the Lincoln Memorial. There was no denying the persuasive political power of that moment.

Just three weeks later, on September 15, 1963, I was horrified when I heard on the news that four black girls had been murdered in a Sunday morning bombing at the Sixteenth Street Baptist Church in Birmingham. I grieved for those girls, three of whom were fourteen years old and the other, who was eleven. When I saw their pictures, I couldn't get their faces out of my head. I kept seeing them smiling, dressed in their Sunday best, unaware of what hit them when the bomb went off. I remembered that kind of terror. I could even smell the dynamite. I knew that the same fate so easily could have been mine.

That same chilling thought raced through my mind again on November 22 when President John F. Kennedy was assassinated. Again, I was devastated. He had seemed so decent on civil rights, and I was looking forward to voting for him the following year. It was to be my first time ever voting. Now President Kennedy was gone, his life extinguished by the same kind of hatred that had been so rampant in Little Rock.

For a while, I felt overloaded—by the tumultuous times, by my state of mind, by the pressures of trying to work full-time and go to school. I told no one in Denver about my background in Little Rock. I even kept my distance from the two local NAACP chapters. I wasn't ready to become a mascot. I didn't want any reminders of my past. I was disappointed in myself. I knew that I wasn't living up to my potential.

Things began to look up for me in 1965 when I came up with a plan to finish college. I needed to get a better job, save money, and attend school full-time so I could focus solely on my studies. I got an interview at the Rocky Flats Plant, a federal nuclear weapons production facility near Denver. I figured there would be a routine background check of some kind, but I was stunned when Daddy came in one evening and told me that the FBI had been in the neighborhood asking questions about me. My heart rate sped up, and I broke out in a sweat. Suddenly, I flashed back to 1960 when FBI agents took my father away. It had been my only experience with the agency. Why would the FBI be involved with my background check?

Shortly thereafter, I received a call from a federal agent. He informed me that I needed to come answer some questions that involved private information about my application for a government job. That made me even more nervous—almost nervous enough to skip the interview. But I needed the job.

When I arrived at the interview, the agent began

peppering me with questions: Did I know this person from Michigan State? Did I join that Communist group? Had I participated in a certain rally at the university? He also asked about some of my associations in Little Rock. I felt jittery inside, but I kept my answers short and truthful.

"Not to my knowledge," I responded each time.

It was clear that the agency had kept a file on me. I gathered that it was because of my role in integrating Central High School. The suspicion sent a chill up my spine. Many years later, in the mid-1970s, news broke that J. Edgar Hoover indeed had kept files filled with personal information on public figures, political and civil rights leaders, particularly those with whom he disagreed.

Whatever is in my file must not have appeared too threatening, though, because I got the job at the Rocky Flats Plant. I stuck to my plan and worked for six months, putting away practically all my salary. I decided to apply to Colorado State College (now called the University of Northern Colorado) in nearby Greeley. The tuition was reasonable, and I wouldn't lose any of my credits from Michigan State.

In addition to the money I had saved, I applied for scholarships. Mrs. Bates sent along a check for a scholarship I had received from the NAACP, for which I was grateful. I also applied for a federal student loan through the Denver National Bank, where I had small savings and checking accounts. I didn't know whether I would get it, as a young black woman. But after some back-and-forthing with the bank's president, I got the loan. It was a small victory but an important one. I felt a spark of the old Carlotta, the determined and focused Carlotta.

Finally, I was grabbing the reins of my life.

# CHAPTER 14

## A Season of Loss

When I saw Grandpa Cullins at a family reunion in Kansas City at the end of summer in 1965, he didn't look well. He seemed thinner and slower than I remembered. I hadn't seen him in the six years since I'd left Little Rock, and a bit of the fire in him had gone out. For the first time, Grandpa Cullins seemed to me like an old man.

The following spring, a telephone call brought dreaded news: Grandpa Cullins had died. He hadn't been feeling well for days, family members said. Then, he went to sleep one night and never woke up. The news filled me with sorrow and regret. Grandpa had been a big presence in my life, but I wished I had not been so intimidated by him. Even with all he had taught me, I knew I could have learned so much more. But it was time to say goodbye for good.

Grieving Grandpa Cullins knocked the wind out of me. Gathering with family for his funeral was healing for all of us, just getting to be all together to honor him. And I had to keep my head up. I was almost done with college, and all I wanted was to graduate and be done with school.

I had to get two part-time jobs to pay my tuition. Each morning, I drove my Volkswagen Bug fifty miles to school in Greeley, Colorado, returned to Denver in the afternoon, and went to back-to-back jobs. I spent most of my downtime studying.

Graduation was just a month away when I turned on the television before heading out to school one morning in April 1968 and heard an astonishing news report: Dr. King had been gunned down on the balcony of a Memphis hotel. By then, I had moved to a Denver apartment within the boundaries of one of the top junior high schools in the state so that my sister Tina could attend, and she stayed with me during the week. The two of us stared, aghast, at the television screen as the announcer reported that King was dead. I didn't want to believe my ears. I felt great sadness for the country, but even more for Dr. King's wife and children, whose loss would be the greatest of all. Racial hatred was still burning wildly across America, and now it had consumed a giant.

I graduated in May from Colorado State. Mother and my two sisters attended the ceremony, but Daddy had to work, which was fine with me. I was just relieved to be finished. Now I could move on, knowing at least that I had completed what I set out to do.

In the aftermath of Dr. King's murder, America was at a time of great unrest. Another fighter for freedom and justice was gone. White supremacists seemed determined to destroy the strongest voices for racial justice. And new, defiant black voices like the Black Panthers were emerging to fight back. They would be punished for doing so; many were spied on by the FBI, incarcerated, and even killed.

I wondered if the country could ever find its way to true peace.

Amid all the national chaos, I applied for a newly created position at the Metropolitan Denver YWCA as program administrator for teenagers. I got the job and went to work for a wonderful woman, Polly Bullard, the executive director, who over the years would become a friend and mentor.

The following September, I married my boyfriend of three years, Ira (Ike) LaNier. We had a small ceremony in the chapel of my church on Friday the thirteenth. I joked that if it didn't work out, we'd have something to blame. We had met for the first time at a house party on Thanksgiving night in 1962. He had just finished college and was working as a substitute teacher. He likes to tell a story about how he had scoped me out—"the tall, lanky one"—from the moment I walked in the door with a couple of my friends.

He declares he had noticed me a month earlier on the public bus route we both took to work but that I had gotten away before he had a chance to make his move. Now at the party was his chance, he says, so he arranged for his roommate to play a certain slow Temptations song as he walked over and asked me to dance. Instead, his roommate decided to play a joke and dropped a James Brown hit. By then, Ike says, he had already asked me to dance and was doing his best to mask his flaw: He couldn't dance a lick, at least not fast.

According to him, I grew bored within a few seconds, waved him off, and preened off the dance floor as he stood there, thoroughly embarrassed, watching his friends cackle with laughter. Of course, I don't remember things that way at all.

When we met again in March 1965, Ike had just returned from military service. His roommate—the same guy who had played the joke on him—was having a house party and invited me and some of my friends. Ike hadn't wanted to see me again after I'd brushed him off. But after having a couple of drinks, Ike says, he walked over, reintroduced himself, told me what I had done when we'd first met, and was preparing to give me a piece of his mind about my rude, arrogant manner, when I stole his thunder. He says I told him that I didn't remember the party but that if he remembered the events of the night that way, it must have happened and that I was sorry for treating him so badly. Apparently, I was different from what Ike had imagined: kinder, more considerate. And we discovered we had some things in common, particularly golf.

I drove Ike home after the party. He didn't even have a car, but every time he tells this story, he complains about how I scared him half to death in my "raggedy" Volkswagen Bug. Anyhow, he invited me in with a promise to cook breakfast and put some jazz on his new stereo. His roommates and their girlfriends soon joined us. Ike says he was trying to impress me during our hours-long conversation in the wee hours of the morning when he asked if I liked golf. He had been a caddy in his hometown of Columbus, Mississippi, and he was hoping to introduce me to the sport. I told him simply that I enjoyed golf. He invited me out to play right then, about five thirty a.m. I accepted, and by the time we drove back to my place to pick up my clubs, City Park course was preparing to open. Of course, I whipped him. He says I had purposely left out that I was a member of the East Denver Golf Club and had been winning tournaments. In any case, I wanted to give him a chance to finally beat me, so the two of us began playing golf together every day. We also found that we both liked other sports as well. I was even the first woman allowed to join the regular Sunday morning football gathering of Ike and his boys. I kept up with them easily. Anyhow, I won Ike over.

He won me over, too. He was taller than me, which was hard to find, and he was a southerner with Mississippi roots. I'd always heard that a southern boy makes a good husband, one devoted to taking care of his wife and children. I realize that's a stereotype, but it's a good one that stuck in the back of my mind. Most of all, he made me laugh. He still does. Nobody can spin a story like Ike.

I don't think I ever really told him that I was one of the Little Rock Nine. He says a friend mentioned it to him—how a friend would have known, I don't know. But growing up in Mississippi, Ike remembered watching television footage of my eight comrades and me. He said that when his friend mentioned my background, he remembered the television footage he had seen as a teenager, and it made him furious all over again. It also made him want to protect me. But I never mentioned my experience at Central, so he didn't, either. More than a decade would pass before circumstances would force us to have that conversation, and by then we were parents.

Our firstborn, a son, Whitney, was born June 25, 1971, followed by our second child, a daughter, Brooke, in 1974. By then, I had left the Y and gotten my real estate license. My real estate career worked well with my family life. I went to work for a woman-owned real estate company near my house. I found that I knew more than I realized about housing construction after having spent so much of my life around men who had made a living in the industry. I spoke their language, which surprised many of the men I encountered in the then male-dominated real estate and construction industries.

My life was stable and happy, and then the bottom fell out.

In late February 1976, Daddy came down with what appeared to be the flu. He had been healthy for most of his life, but he didn't go to the doctor regularly. In recent months, I'd noticed that he seemed tired all the time. Daddy was hospitalized one February day after his temperature shot up to 106 degrees. He also complained of muscle aches. But he still looked healthy, so I figured he would be back on his feet soon enough. I visited Daddy at the hospital every day. When nearly two weeks passed and he didn't seem to be getting any better, I grew worried. Then came a frightening diagnosis: Daddy had leukemia.

Mother tried to keep a positive attitude. Everything would turn out okay, she assured herself and me. But Daddy seemed sad and exhausted.

I called Loujuana, who was living in Pennsylvania, and she came back to Denver right away. Before our littlest sister, Tina, arrived, Daddy slipped into a coma. As shocking as it was to see him lying there, unable to communicate, he looked as if he were just asleep. That gave us something to hang on to. He hadn't lost weight. His color looked good. We all remained confident that he would pull through.

On March 2, I spent the entire day at the hospital, mostly just sitting quietly with Daddy and chatting with other family members as they came and went. I left for the night about nine p.m., made it home, and peeked at my sleeping toddler and preschooler. I was just about to climb into bed about an hour or so later when I received a call from the hospital. Daddy had experienced unexpected complications, and doctors were not able to save him.

I felt weak, but my mind rebelled: I'd just left Daddy; I was planning to see him again in the morning; I didn't even say goodbye; what do you mean he's gone? Suddenly, I was that heartbroken little girl again, longing for her daddy to come home.

I could have stayed curled in my bed forever. But through my tears I saw Mother, scarcely able to comprehend burying the fifty-three-year-old love of her life. My sisters were no better. And things needed to get done. Somehow, I pulled myself together enough to make the arrangements. Mother wondered whether we should return to Little Rock to bury Daddy, but I knew he wouldn't want that. We decided to bury him near us in Fort Logan National Cemetery in Denver.

A spring snow covered the ground as my family and

close friends gathered at Fort Logan for the military burial. Daddy would have appreciated the dignity of the service. Crisply dressed military men firing their rifles in a unified three-gun salute. A bugler hitting every mournful note of "Taps." And the U.S. flag folded to perfection and presented to Mother.

Time stopped there for Daddy and me. And then I faced the most difficult moment of my life: turning away and walking into the rest of my days without him.

# CHAPTER 15

## Finding My Voice

Soon after Daddy died, I received a letter from Elizabeth Huckaby, the former vice principal for girls at Central. She was working on a book about that tumultuous 1957–1958 school year, and she wanted some input from my eight comrades and me. I read the letter and put it aside. Those memories were buried deep in my past. I didn't want to relive them. I never responded to Mrs. Huckaby's letter. It had nothing to do with her. I just couldn't.

I didn't hear any more about the project until 1981, when I heard advertisements for the made-for-television movie *Crisis at Central High*. The movie was based on Mrs. Huckaby's manuscript, and it was about to air on CBS. By then, Ike's job had relocated us to Atlanta, and the children were in school there. Just days before the movie was scheduled to air, I talked to Ike, who agreed that we needed to have a family meeting. Whitney was in the fourth grade then, old enough to understand; Brooke was just six. We sat down together as a family, and Ike and I talked to them about the Little Rock Nine, my role, and the movie that was about to air. On the night of the movie, we planned to watch it together, but I couldn't sit still. I was fidgeting, and I kept leaving the room, trying to push away any old emotions. Ike was teary-eyed. Whitney heard my name.

"Mommy, is that you?" he asked.

It was a young actress pretending to be me when I was a little girl, I explained. He was full of questions: Why did the people look so mean? Why were they saying those things to me and my friends? Was I scared?

Brooke was quieter and less curious about the movie, which suited me just fine. But I answered Whitney's questions. I kept my answers short, child-appropriate, and unemotional. Whitney would be in high school, and our family would be back in Denver before we ever discussed Central High School again.

But after putting the children to bed, I thought about what I had seen on television. I thought the movie had done a good job of capturing the tension and upheaval of that awful year. It was told through Mrs. Huckaby's eyes, centering a white teacher, not us. I thought the Hollywood character was a bit too compassionate. I respected Mrs. Huckaby because she was fair and efficient.

She tracked down the troublemakers who could be identified, and punished them—which drew the rage of the segregationists. But I never sensed from her the warmth I saw in the Hollywood version of the story.

In the days after the movie, I heard from a few friends, mostly those who already knew my story. They said they were amazed by what we went through and didn't believe they could have put up with that kind of treatment. But the buzz over the movie soon died down, and I again pushed Central out of my mind.

Mother and I didn't discuss the movie either. She, too, was reluctant to talk about the painful parts of our past. But she maintained close ties to Little Rock. She traveled there more frequently than I, and each summer, she met up with old friends from that time. I occasionally accompanied Mother there. Sometimes, I saw Mrs. Monts, Herbert's mother, by then a retired special education teacher. She always updated me on the accomplishments of her nine children. But when she got to her oldest son, her face lit up as she said: "But I'm especially proud of Herbert. . . ." He had gotten married, moved to Detroit, and was working in the automotive industry, she said.

I knew what I needed to know: that Herbert had refused to let the trouble in Little Rock ruin his life. For years, that knowledge was enough. It brought me comfort to know that he was all right, that he had somehow found a way to move on.

I thought I had moved on, too. I had opened my own business as a real estate broker and was volunteering as a board member of the Colorado AIDS Project. This was the 1980s, when AIDS was a mysterious disease sweeping through the country, wiping out primarily young gay men and others in the prime of their lives. Hysteria over the disease was so rampant that our organization didn't even put the address of our headquarters on letters because we feared it might be bombed. I was eager to try to help relieve the suffering when I saw so many young people dying throughout the country. Discrimination against the gay community was widespread, and those suffering from the disease were often forced from their homes and jobs and abandoned by family members and friends. Our group ran a food pantry and provided case management and a volunteer "buddy" to those who needed companionship and help determining and balancing their health-care needs. Through my work on the board, I found a way to fight injustice. Few knew just how much my own past helped me identify with those who were hurting.

I'd soon learn, though, that burying a painful past doesn't necessarily mean you've moved beyond it. It's often still there, simmering, waiting for some unexpected moment to erupt, spewing forth every hurtful thing that you thought had gone away. That's what happened in

1987, when the Little Rock Nine gathered in Little Rock as guests of the NAACP for the thirtieth anniversary of our landmark school desegregation fight. It was an emotional reunion because it was the first time that all nine of us had come together since Central. I'd seen Ernie regularly at Michigan State and stayed in contact with him on and off afterward. I'd seen Terry, Jefferson, and Melba once or twice over the years, too.

But keeping those memories buried would be more difficult in Little Rock. I hadn't been back to Central since I graduated. At first, it felt good to see so much positive change. The student body president of Central—a black boy—greeted the nine of us in the classroom that had served as the chapel and a haven for us in the morning before class thirty years earlier. We also were welcomed home by the new black mayor, Lottie Shackelford, who had been in Ernie's class at Horace Mann. But when we moved into the freshly scrubbed halls, I couldn't escape the old ghosts. The noise, the angry white faces, the slimy spit—they were right there in my face. The next thing I knew, the usually cool, calm, and collected Carlotta was outside, gasping for air, unable to stop the tears from flowing. I knew then that there would be no stuffing all of that hurt back inside. I had to find a way to make peace with my past.

First and most important, I reconnected with my eight

comrades for good. The nine of us spent hours together, catching up on our post-Central lives—our families, careers, and future plans. We exchanged telephone numbers and addresses and promised to stay in touch—a promise I'm proud to say we've kept. There are only eight other people in this world who know exactly what happened to us at Central and how it felt. It helped to be able to pick up the telephone and call one of them on a particularly bad day. It felt good to share our evolving lives.

When I returned from Little Rock, I began getting calls from longtime friends, acquaintances, and even neighbors in Denver who had seen a report about the reunion on CNN. They all wanted to know: Why didn't you tell us?

"I've known you twenty years, and you never said a word," one friend told me.

They all assumed I was just being humble. But that wasn't it. There were no words for how desperately I had needed to forget.

Several strangers looked up my number in the telephone directory and invited me to speak in their churches, communities, and schools. I ignored the invitations. But one history teacher was particularly persistent. She taught at Ponderosa High School in Parker, Colorado, and she kept calling. We were peers, she said. She remembered the stories about the Little Rock Nine, and this would be a way to make history come alive for her students. A reporter at the Denver *Rocky Mountain News* would be sitting in the class when I spoke.

I didn't have a canned speech and just talked to the students from my heart. I tried to connect by reminding them that I was their age when I made the decision to attend Central. One boy told me my story sounded surreal. There was no way they would not have fought back, several of them said. I talked to them about what life was like for southern black folks at that time. We were expected to maintain our dignity, no matter what. We just had to have faith that justice would prevail. I'd like to think I helped the students put a face on a story they had read in a book and helped them to understand the human toll. But even more, I hope I left them with the message that true heroism starts with one brave decision to do the right thing.

I hope I helped them to understand that diversity is at least a two-way street. It doesn't belong only on the shoulders of black children and their families. White families who believe in the ideals of a multiracial society have to be willing to make some tough choices and sacrifices, too.

One day my son Whitney's friend read a story about the Little Rock Nine and saw a picture of me.

"Isn't this your mom?" he asked Whitney.

When Whitney confirmed that the photo was me,

the friend asked if I could come to their school to speak. Whitney rushed home with the invitation. I agreed. I was accepting speaking engagements more frequently. Maybe it would gradually become easier, I thought. But the opposite was true. The more I talked about Central and Little Rock, the more I remembered, and the tougher it got. From time to time, a new memory would come forth from some long-hidden place, and the tears would start to flow. The flashbacks and tears were scary to me at first, given my tendency toward staying strong. But I kept going, kept speaking.

I also tried to stay close to Big Daddy, who in 1995 turned one hundred years old. For his birthday, my sisters and I traveled to the Department of Veterans Affairs home in Seattle, where Big Daddy was living at the time. The staff had a big birthday party for him, and he seemed to be happy. His health was failing, though. Big Daddy had been suffering from dementia for years and had been forced to close his businesses in Little Rock.

He had always wanted to live to be 100. On May 1, 1997, Big Daddy slipped away, having lived to see 102. I was in awe of him.

The year before Big Daddy died, I got word that the city of Little Rock was planning a huge commemoration for the fortieth anniversary of the integration of Central. There was vigorous debate about it. Was a celebration appropriate? The local chapter of the NAACP argued that it seemed more like a public relations stunt than a meaningful apology. But I thought it was a good idea to recognize the fortieth anniversary. I wanted to see Little Rock acknowledge its past, as ugly as it was. I also saw it as a positive step that the city wanted to showcase how much had indeed changed.

I called my eight comrades so we could discuss. As I saw it, the time had come for us to take as much control as possible of our own legacy. We needed to do what we could to assure that we were informing the next generation about the Little Rock Nine and the importance of education.

I pitched the idea of starting the Little Rock Nine Foundation. Through the foundation, we could give back to the community as a group and continue the journey that we had started so many years ago toward academic excellence and equity.

We agreed to start the foundation. We also agreed that we would participate as a group in the fortieth anniversary commemoration.

The commemoration was as big as we had imagined, with a week of receptions, lectures, honors, and appearances. It drew many dignitaries, including President Bill Clinton, who was himself an Arkansas native son.

Of all the wonderful events that week, the image in my head of the ceremony on September 25, 1997—exactly forty years after we first marched up the front steps into

Central—will stay with me forever. Thousands of people of all races, local residents as well as guests from all over the world, assembled at Central to welcome the nine of us home. They applauded and stood to their feet as we were presented. Then we ascended the steps to the front entrance of our alma mater. President Clinton and Governor Mike Huckabee were waiting there and held open the door for us—a gesture that touched all of us deeply. Forty years earlier, we had entered those doors under the protection of gun-toting federal troopers, against the will of the state's segregationist governor. Now the president of the United States stood at the door to usher us through. There were few dry eyes among us. This time, though, I was shedding tears of joy.

It was good to see Mrs. Bates during the festivities. I hadn't seen her in many years. She was in a wheelchair, but she looked well. I'd heard that she had fallen on difficult financial times and even faced the threat of losing her home after the death of Mr. Bates in 1980. That saddened and frustrated me, and I did what I could to help when Ernie rallied to try to save the home where so much of our history had taken place. It eventually was declared a National Historic Landmark maintained by the National Park Service, which allowed it to remain a private residence. When I saw her at the reception, I walked over and embraced her.

I felt good about how well the nine of us were doing

in our lives. We were raising families, giving back to our communities, and enjoying success in our various careers. I had been in business as an independent real estate broker for the past twenty years. Coolheaded Ernie had earned a master's degree in sociology, had worked in President Jimmy Carter's administration, and was rising in the finance industry at Lehman Brothers. He was based in Washington, DC.

Melba, who seemed born for the spotlight, had earned a graduate degree in journalism from Columbia University, worked as a reporter for NBC-TV and a communications consultant, and had recently authored a successful memoir about her experiences at Central. She was living in San Francisco.

Gloria, the brainy one, had graduated from the Illinois Institute of Technology with a degree in math and chemistry and moved to Sweden to work as a systems analyst and technical writer for IBM as well as a patent attorney for IBM and editor of *Computers in Industry* magazine.

Terrence, a philosopher and professor long before he got the degrees to back it up, earned a bachelor's in sociology from California State University, a master's in social welfare from UCLA, and a doctorate in psychology from Southern Illinois University. He was living and working in Los Angeles as a college professor and clinical psychologist.

Jefferson, the perpetual jokester of the group, had

earned a bachelor's degree in business administration from Los Angeles State College, served in Vietnam, and was working as a government accountant in Columbus, Ohio.

Minnijean, who had become famously known for fighting back that first year at Central with the so-called chili incident, attended Southern Illinois University and moved to a farm in Ottawa, Canada, with her husband and six children. She worked as a writer and social worker and got involved in grassroots human rights groups.

Thelma, quiet and fragile because of a heart condition, had earned bachelor's and master's degrees in education from Southern Illinois University. She worked twenty-seven years as a home economics teacher in St. Louis before retiring in 1994.

And then there was Elizabeth, who had been the most scarred among us by the events of 1957. The image of her all alone, surrounded by the shrieking mob, has endured more than any other as a testament of the courage it took to survive that year. She attended college in Tennessee and Ohio and served in the army before returning to Little Rock to work for a state welfare agency. But Elizabeth struggled mightily to find her way out of the darkness of the past. When we gathered for the anniversary, it was clear to me she was still battling old ghosts.

The nine of us had agreed with *Newsweek* magazine

to be interviewed for a cover story about the anniversary. But once we got there, Elizabeth suddenly backed out. The reporter turned to me for help in changing her mind. I went to talk to her. We needed to do this for a number of reasons, I told her, but most importantly because we wanted to tell our own stories and set the historical record straight.

"Carlotta, I just don't think I can get through it," Elizabeth responded.

"I know how you feel," I told her. "But if I sit with you, will you do it?"

She agreed. Melba also offered to sit with her for the interview. In an empty banquet room at the Excelsior Hotel, Melba and I sat on each side of Elizabeth and almost had to hold her up as she recalled that terrifying moment when she found herself alone, surrounded by a threatening white mob.

After the fortieth reunion, the honors kept coming. Just two years later, President Clinton presented the award in the White House that Congress had bestowed on us, the Congressional Gold Medal.

But four days before we were set to travel to the nation's capital to accept the award, I received a call from Ernie, who had bad news: Mrs. Bates had died. Mrs. Bates would want us to accept the award, we figured. When we were kids, she had escorted us to many such events herself. Ernie came up with a solution: He would fly to Little Rock the morning of the funeral and represent us before returning to Washington in time for the medal ceremony.

The following April, we all attended a memorial service for Mrs. Bates in Little Rock. The service drew an overflow crowd of local and national political and civil rights leaders, as well as local residents who remembered the woman who had dared to stand up to Jim Crow. This time, my comrades asked me to speak on behalf of our group.

In my speech, I recalled how Mrs. Bates had hired me as a ten-year-old "paperboy" to deliver her and her husband's *Arkansas State Press*. I recalled how she used the newspaper as a megaphone to protest the injustices endured by the black community. I talked about our transition from news messengers to newsmakers as the story of the Little Rock Nine played out around the world. I also thanked her for the role she had played in bravely supporting the nine of us and our parents—even in the face of hatred and violence.

"Mrs. Bates 'walked the talk' of freedom for all, strode confidently forward, aware of the dangers she faced but determined to see the walls of segregation come tumbling down," I said. "This is the Daisy Bates that the Little Rock Nine remembers. This is the woman who put her life on the line for the cause of justice. This is the American whose vision for educational equality moved our nation forward."

As I took my seat, I thought about the irony of the moment. While we were at Central, I would have been the last one Mrs. Bates asked to speak for the group. She knew I shunned the limelight. But here I stood, before an esteemed crowd, bidding a final farewell to the one who for many years had spoken for my comrades and me.

Here I stood, on my own, speaking for us all, finally confident in the voice emerging from within.

# CHAPTER 16

## Peace at Last

**E**ven after years of talking to students and other groups about Central High School, I had a difficult time discussing the bombing of my family's home. Every time I mentioned how my father had been held by the police, I choked up. It was just as tough to talk about what had happened to Herbert.

I still blamed myself for it all. But the deeper I dug into my past, the more difficult it was to avoid the questions: Why Herbert? How did he end up in the hands of Little Rock police? How long did he stay in prison? What happened to him there? How did he get out? What was his life like now?

A piece of my life had intertwined forever with Herbert's on that fateful night in February 1960. I had come to realize that to make peace with my own past, I first had to face it. All of it. That meant facing Herbert, too. I decided to call him.

First, I called his younger brother, Dr. Lester Monts, to get Herbert's telephone number. Then, while I was seeing family in Chicago in August 2003, I made the call.

It was good to hear his voice. I explained to him that I had been thinking a lot about Little Rock and what happened to my family's home and told him that I wanted to talk to him. I asked if I could drive to his home in Michigan to talk face-to-face. Herbert seemed happy to hear from me and agreed without hesitation to get together. The next day, I drove four and a half hours to Southfield, just outside Detroit, where Herbert had been living the past fifteen years.

When I arrived in town, I called Herbert, and he met me on the highway and led me to his home. I felt proud of him as I drove through his neighborhood, an upscale suburban community with towering old trees, manicured lawns, and large homes. Southfield was widely known throughout Michigan as home to many of the area's prominent black politicians, including the town's first black mayor and several council members.

We were met inside by Herbert's wife of more than forty years, Dora, a manager for a major department store. A warm and friendly woman, she broke the ice right away and insisted that I stay overnight at their home, instead of in a hotel as I had planned. The three of us sat in the family room and chatted amiably about Little Rock and family for a couple of hours, and then she headed upstairs to bed.

Herbert and I kept talking, first about work. He had worked thirty-three years as an officer for the United Auto Workers union in various roles. In his union work, it seemed Herbert had found a noble purpose, a way to help protect the average worker from multimillion-dollar corporate giants. The job meant more than a paycheck to him, he said, because he knew better than most what it was like to be defenseless in the face of power.

Then Herbert steered our conversation to Little Rock and the night in 1960 when both our lives changed forever.

"I had nothing to do with it," he said softly, as if he needed me to hear him say it.

"I know," I answered.

I wasn't quite sure what to say next. But Herbert needed no prompting. He had been waiting all these years for the chance to tell me what happened. It seemed that he needed to talk about it as much as I needed to hear it. So, for hours that night, I just listened.

In that conversation and the many since, I've let Herbert take me back to Little Rock, 1960, starting with that stormy evening of February 9:

Our hangout back then was your grandfather's place, at the corner of Eighteenth and Pine . . . I was there with Charles Webb and Marion Davis, some neighborhood buddies. Maceo came by; he was my uncle's friend. It was a rainy evening, and 'long about nine or ten, Charles, Marion, and I started out for our homes. We walked up Pine, cut across an alley, and Charles went on into his home on Seventeenth. Then, Marion and I continued up Maple to Fifteenth, and he went into his home.

I passed your home and noticed a couple of unfamiliar, early-1950s cars on the street. I walked on to my house just up the street. Maceo passed me in his car and turned the corner in front of your house, onto Valentine. He was behind a truck, another unfamiliar vehicle in the neighborhood. We knew the cars and trucks of our neighbors, so it was easy to tell a stranger on the roads.

I got home within five to ten minutes after Marion went to his house. My dad was at work. He worked nights at Bell Telephone. I had two sisters, six brothers, and my mom at home. I ate a bite, saw there was nothing of interest on television, and went on to bed.

I guess it was maybe fifteen minutes at the most.

I was about to fall off to sleep when I heard a big boom. I got up quickly, went to my mother, and said: "Did you hear that?" We had had a big rain—and there was a red clay residue that had left puddles around. I looked out the window and saw a police car parked on the corner. At the time, it never crossed my mind to wonder how a police car could get there more quickly than I could get out of my bed and look out the window.

People were gathering at the Rices' house. I told my mother I was going on down there to see what had happened. The police came over to the Rices' and told us to stand back. We all knew that you were at Central, and we all figured that the white segregationists had come to pay a call.

The police suggested we break up the gathering and go on back to our homes. I went on home and back to bed.

When I woke up the next morning, I went outside to see what was going on. The police car was still there. I went down and told the officer that I had seen several unfamiliar cars in the neighborhood when I was walking home last night.

"We'll send somebody out to talk with you," he told me.

The police came to my house the next morning, and I remember going down to headquarters and telling my story. I went by myself. They took my story, but it became clear to me that they wanted something else from me. They wanted me to take a lie detector test. I didn't have anything to hide, so I agreed. They let me go home and picked me up again the next morning. I went by myself because I thought I'd take the lie detector test and come on back home. But things began to change. They started asking me the same questions again and again. It was night before I took the lie detector test, and I passed it. I clearly heard one of the officers say, "There's nothing there."

They got Marion to come down to the station, too. Later, I found out that most of the people on Eighteenth and Pine were also questioned. Police tried to get some of them involved, but they had substantial evidence backing their whereabouts that night.

After I volunteered to take the lie detector test, I requested an attorney. It was clear they were looking for a fall guy.

"You guys are trying to railroad me. Get me an attorney," I told them.

That's when I got charged.

During the questioning, the police were telling me that Maceo had already confessed. I found out later that they were telling Maceo that I had confessed.

Whatever I said, they would counter with: "Boy, you are lying."

Earzie Cunningham, who lived next door to the Foxes, across the street from you, told the police that he had seen me on the street by your house. Earzie was in trouble with the law, and they coerced him into putting me by your house at the time of the explosion. He lied. His mother even said he did not see anything, but the prosecutor, Frank Holt, found out about her statement. Before she could be subpoenaed to testify, Holt claimed that she had a heart condition and that medical reasons made it not feasible for her to testify. Word was she was whisked out of town, under a threat.

The police kept saying to me: "Did you

register to go to Central? Didn't you go to school in Connecticut for a while? Aren't those schools integrated?"

All of these questions I could answer in the affirmative, but they kept repeating the questions as though my "yes" answers annoyed them.

I had been there all day and into the night by this time, and it was the usual treatment for blacks back then—no bathroom breaks, no food, no water. They would not let me call my parents. I kept repeating my request for a lawyer. As soon as I did, they charged me with the crime and started to beat me. The FBI agents were federal employees, but it is important to remember that in Little Rock they were also, for the most part, southern white men. They were every bit as bad as the police, just as racist as the locals. They weren't there for justice. They were on the side of the segregationists. When I asked for a lawyer, which I did repeatedly, Frank Holt came into the room, but this was after they had prepared a confession. He was the prosecuting attorney, and no help to me. In fact, he wanted me to take the fall, and it was his plan to make that happen.

I didn't see Police Chief Gene Smith until the next morning. I knew Chief Smith because I mowed the yard of one of his neighbors, and he would come over to talk with me and my friends when we were in the neighborhood. This morning, however, he made like he didn't even know me.

"I had nothing to do with the bombing," I told him.

But he was so determined. And determined to get somebody black, it seemed to me. During this marathon day with the authorities, and after I had asked for an attorney, which I kept doing, they would beat on me, three and four at a time.

They had prepared a confession. I kept asking for an attorney. I never got an attorney, but they were successful in breaking me. I signed something.

The next day I was arraigned, along with Maceo, who apparently was somewhere in the station, but in a different room. At the arraignment, Mr. Bates came down and told me I was being railroaded, that whatever was going on was just a smoke screen to throw shame onto blacks.

After I had been arraigned and bail was

set, Dr. Routen, a prominent black physician, covered my bail for me. He put up his property, knowing that I wouldn't skip out. I would show. It was my own word, and I would honor Dr. Routen's trust in me.

The trial, it was a kangaroo court. Every black person in the courtroom knew it. But it was my life that was being railroaded, nobody else's. I knew I was in trouble when Judge Kirby got impatient at one point when the jury left the room. He turned to the bailiff and said aloud:

"Get that convicting jury back in here! We don't have any more time to waste."

My attorney turned to me and said, "Oh my, you don't stand a chance. Did you hear what the judge said?"

That was it. I was sentenced to five years, the maximum allowed for the charge.

I reported to Cummins State Farm in October 1961. It was a working farm. The one thing you didn't want was a job harvesting cotton. They ran that part like a plantation; it was legalized slavery. But I had some connections; my uncle was able to get me a job that wasn't a part of the farm work. Blacks were often given the job of cooking or driving.

I was a driver and would often make trips off-site to run errands in Pine Bluff for the officials.

I wasn't doing any of the hard labor . . . Because Cummins wasn't that far from Little Rock, I had visitors. My family stayed supportive.

I always believed I would be able to get out. In high school, I used to work part-time as a waiter at the country club, and a lot of powerful politicians and attorneys used to come in there. I thought one of them might be able to help.

But one afternoon my daddy was downtown, and he ran into Charles Bussey. Everybody knew him. He became mayor of Little Rock in 1981, but back then, he was a black deputy sheriff, and he had real good political connections. He asked about me, and Daddy told him I was still in jail for the bombing. Everybody knew that I didn't do it. Bussey said he would arrange a meeting with Governor Faubus, and he did.

My parents went to see the governor. They told him I was still in jail for a crime that I didn't commit. He promised them that he would see to it that I was released. It's kind of ironic that the man who had caused all of this trouble in the first place ended up helping me get out. About three weeks after that, in June 1963, I got out. I got out early. I had a five-year sentence, but I served twenty months of actual jail time.

I was planning to leave Little Rock right away, but everybody I ran into was kind. They all knew I had been railroaded. They knew I was innocent. Little Rock had been my home, so I had lots of friends. It's like a small town, so I was bound to run into the people who had put me behind bars. I saw Earzie Cunningham going up Oak Street one day in our old neighborhood. He pulled his car up beside me and apologized. I said to him, "Why did you lie about me?" He told me that they pressured him, that he could have been arrested for something he had done, but he made a deal.

Not long after that, I took my car to be serviced, and I ran into Frank Holt. I went up to him and said: "You convicted me of something I didn't do."

My last words to him were something along the lines of "So, that's what you call police brutality."

Still later, one Sunday morning when I
went to get a newspaper, I saw Judge Kirby.

"Why don't you come to my office? I have
some things I want to discuss with you," he
said.

Judge Kirby knew I was innocent, but that
line about the "convicting jury" made me
want to stay as far from him as I could. I didn't
trust him, not one bit.

I ended up staying in Little Rock longer
than I thought I would. A plumber who
belonged to the church my family attended . . .
hired me to work for him. Then, in 1963, a
friend of mine introduced me to Dora. She was
from Jackson, Mississippi, but she was living
in Little Rock. We hit it off, and three years
later, we got married. Another friend of mine
had moved to Detroit and liked it. He told me
job opportunities were wide open there. I had
an uncle who lived there, and he promised to
help me get a job in the automobile industry.
I just felt like there was something better
out there. So in August 1968, I packed up and
moved to Detroit. I found a job at a General
Motors subsidiary in Livonia, Michigan. We've
been here ever since.

I got involved in the union 'long about
1972. Vietnam veterans were returning from
the war to their old jobs in the General Motors
plants, and they felt like the union didn't
really represent them. They were in a different
mood, rebellious. They wanted change. Most
of the people in office were older. Some of
my friends and co-workers encouraged me
to run for office, so I did. I was elected as
an alternate on the committee that handled
grievances, health and safety issues for the
union. In the next election, I was elected a
full member to the committee. I went to work
for the union full-time, and I just kept rising
through the ranks from there.

Although I'm retired, I still get called on
from time to time to do work for the union,
and every now and then, I volunteer for
political campaigns. I'm a grandfather now,
too. My son, Rod, is a journalist. He got a
master's degree from Wayne State in Detroit
and worked as an editor for NBC Online. Now,
he and his wife own a public relations firm.

It's kind of funny how life works out,
because I used to want to go into journalism
when I was in high school. I used to work for

> the school newspaper. My second choice
> was the military. But after everything that
> happened, I didn't really have that chance.
>> Things turned out all right for me, though.
> Yes, things turned out just fine.

Herbert suffered in ways that can never be measured. Dreams died. A seventeen-year-old boy entered manhood behind the bars of a maximum-security state prison and spent the first twenty months of his adult life there.

Somehow, though, Herbert emerged from it all strong and determined. He dreamed new dreams and built a new life—a successful and productive life of service.

For Herbert, that has been vindication enough. For me, knowing his full story and doing what I can to clear his name has helped to bring my soul what I have most sought: peace.

# CHAPTER 17

## Touching the Future

Wherever I go to talk to students, I usually encounter some who know little or nothing about the Little Rock Nine. Sometimes they're black. Sometimes they're white, Latino, or Asian. But when they hear my story, often they get angry, like the white boy whose hand went up slowly in the back of the classroom after my first speech at Ponderosa High School.

"Why am I just learning this?" he asked. "Why haven't I learned this in school before now?"

I hear that often from high school and college students who feel their school systems and parents neglected to share important pieces of American history. I don't blame young people for not knowing. I do blame parents and schools, though. I bear some responsibility as part of a generation that I don't believe has done enough to ensure that our children and their children know and fully appreciate our collective history, particularly the hard-fought battles for African Americans to gain full access to educational opportunities and civil rights.

It distresses me to see that the nation's public schools have largely become resegregated. But even more, I'm disturbed by the low regard for education in many parts of the country. It is hurtful now when I hear that in many urban schools, where the student populations tend to be overwhelmingly black or Latin American, there are still not enough resources for kids to access internet, textbooks, or even pencils—all resources they need in order to learn.

While the problems that plague the poorest among us today—including a lack of education and health care—are indeed complicated, I believe that those of us in a position to help should show solidarity. Together we can go a long way toward getting young people the support they need. We can restore education to its vaunted place—and reconnect students to their own cultural history.

In recent years, the federal government, the state of Arkansas, and some respected artists have made the history of the Little Rock Nine more tangible. There's a touching monument of the nine of us that stands on the north end of the Arkansas State Capitol grounds. Life-size bronze statues, made by editorial cartoonist John Deering and his wife, Kathy, capture each of us as the children we were then, in a memorial simply called

*Testament.* State lawmakers agreed to locate it on the Capitol grounds within view of the governor's office. That made me proud. I'd like to think that whenever the Arkansas governor has to sign a bill, he will think twice about his actions when he glances out his window. There we are, nine bronze statues, staring back at him in a silent testament to history.

In 2008, I was inspired by the hope and optimism President Barack Obama's presidential campaign represented. The day he won the election was a proud day in America—one, I admit, I did not see coming. I'd seen too much hate, the kind that had fueled the white mobs of my youth. The kind that had murdered Dr. King, the Kennedys, and those four little black girls who died in the church bombing in Birmingham. I'd seen, too, the more subtle (but no less destructive) racism and discrimination, the microaggressions that fly below the radar and often make the accuser seem paranoid if they try to raise the issue. The black man always has to do more and prove more, and more times than not, he still falls short in their eyes, my friend Horace Walker would say in his most frustrated moments. I would say the very same goes for black people of any gender.

I'd seen a lot of good, too—genuine color-blind goodness from white men and women who had been able to look me in the eyes and see me for what I am: a woman, a child of God, no more, no less. And the night Obama won, tears streamed down black faces, white faces, brown faces, cream faces. The activist Reverend Jesse Jackson, who had been on the balcony with Dr. King when the fatal shots rang out, looked genuinely overcome with emotion. Strangers were hugging. Horns were honking. Obama signs were flapping. Black news reporters, trained to maintain a poker face, were choking up, talking about their own mothers, fathers, and grandparents.

Before I could even begin to process it all, my phone began ringing off the hook with calls from tearful peers, my sisters, Mother.

Everyone asked the same question: "Can you believe it?"

And then they'd say: "I never thought I'd see this day."

Ike and I were quiet and reflective, two children of the segregated South, perhaps still in a state of shock.

Just before ten p.m. MST, Obama took the stage with his wife and children. Even he seemed somewhat subdued and awed by the magnitude of this victory.

"If there is anyone out there who still doubts that America is a place where all things are possible, who still wonders if the dream of our founders is alive in our time, who still questions the power of our democracy, tonight is your answer."

He was talking to me. The tears began welling inside. Yes, I had my answer. America had proven me wrong—or at least filled in the blank. We were a country in great need of moving beyond its racial scars and wounds into a more hopeful future.

I soaked up every bit of this historic moment—the faces, the cheers, the energy, the joy, the hope for this young man who looked like me. I had seen this country at its worst, and now I was able to see and touch the monumental change unfolding before me.

But in spite of the incredible hope I felt stirring across the country for those eight years, it felt as if it all came crashing down when Donald Trump was elected president. He had campaigned on racist rhetoric—and it worked in his favor.

I wondered, as politicians chipped away at voting rights that would affect black folks across the country: Were we doomed to backslide farther and farther into Jim Crow territory all over again?

But in November 2019, America said no. No to another four years of President Trump. No to the bigotry he seemed to encourage in others. In part, the election outcome came about because of young people; teenagers and college-age kids who were voting for their very first time. The shock and joy of having Vice President Kamala Harris—a mixed-race black woman—in the White House hasn't worn off for me yet.

But with all the progress that has been made over the

last few decades, there is still more to come. And I believe that young people, like I once was at Central, will be the ones to lead the way.

Racist violence still crops up, the same kind I knew so well from my youth—the spitting in the school hallways, the bombing of my home, the beatings Daddy, Herbert, and Maceo had endured at the hands of police. In the summer of 2020, tired and frustrated by the coronavirus, and grieving for the lives of George Floyd, Breonna Taylor, and other slain young black people, people of all races, backgrounds, ethnicities, genders, and religions took to the streets. Hundreds of thousands of them, marching across cities and small towns. It was an extraordinary sight.

I didn't feel aligned with the turbulent protests that made headlines, even if I understood the anger. But I did feel mighty aligned with the countless peaceful protests, rallies, vigils, and memorials that held a torch up for black lives lost. These marches proudly declared that black lives matter while we're still alive, that living a long life with dignity—with access to good health, food, education, and opportunity—is due to all people.

And then, just like that, other nations joined in; people across oceans marched and carried signs in other languages in the name of Black Lives Matter. Across the world, sea after sea of faces could be seen, joining together as allies.

What a long journey it had been from Little Rock and Central to this moment.

As I sat before the television watching news reports about those impromptu, nonviolent protests, my shero Rosa Parks came to mind. With her quiet determination, she had shown me long ago what an ordinary person, of any age, could do. The fact that these marches were packed with young people, teenagers, and children is perhaps what made my eyes sting the most.

When I climbed those steps as a teenager at Central, flanked by federal troopers on that September morning more than fifty years ago, I was just a fourteen-year-old girl doing what felt right for me. In time, I would come to understand the greater good—that my eight comrades and I were helping to start a journey sure to outlast any of us. But even with that knowledge, I could not imagine a future as spectacular as this, with so many people proudly showing their solidarity all together.

I felt grateful to be alive. Now nothing could stop the tears.

Me at about eight years old, around the time I took my first life-changing trip to New York City. *(Photo by M. A. Binns)*

At home with my parents (Cartelyou and Juanita Walls) when I was four years old. *(Photo by Earl Davy)*

Little Rock Central High School, which the National Institute of Architects called "America's Most Beautiful School" when it was built in 1927. *(Courtesy of the author)*

Me, Gloria Ray, Jane Hill (standing behind Gloria), and Ernest Green as we face the National Guard on September 4, 1957, on our first attempt to enter Central; Jane never returned to Central after that day. *(Will Counts Collection: Indiana University Archives)*

NAACP attorney Thurgood Marshall with, from left, Melba, Jefferson, Gloria, Daisy Bates, me, Minnijean, and Elizabeth, on the steps of the U.S. Supreme Court. *(AP Images)*

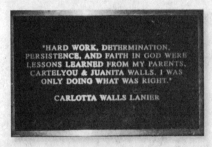

The most relieved member of Central's graduating class of 1960. *(Courtesy of the author)*

"HARD WORK, DETERMINATION, PERSISTENCE, AND FAITH IN GOD WERE LESSONS LEARNED FROM MY PARENTS, CARTELYOU & JUANITA WALLS. I WAS ONLY DOING WHAT WAS RIGHT."

CARLOTTA WALLS LANIER

The plaque next to the bronze depiction of me in the "Testament" memorial that stands on the north end of the Arkansas State Capitol in Little Rock. *(Courtesy of the author)*

The "Testament" memorial features life-size bronze statues of each of the Little Rock Nine. *(Courtesy of the author)*

On August 31, 2005, the United States Postal Service dedicated a 37-cent postage stamp recognizing the Little Rock Nine as part of its "To Form a More Perfect Union" collection. *(Courtesy of the author)*

President Clinton awarded the Little Rock Nine a Congressional Gold Medal in November 1999. *(Courtesy of the author)*

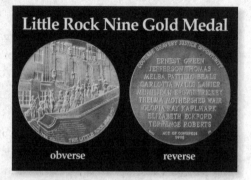

Ernie (far left), Terrence (far right), and me with then-Senator Barack Obama at a Congressional Black Caucus event in 2007. *(Courtesy of Altria Client Services)*

# A NOTE ON SOURCES

This book reflects many years of digging into the depths of my memory, unearthing painful pieces of my history that I buried when I walked away from Central High School in May 1960. After years of prodding me to tell my story for the public record, my friend Dr. Margaret Whitt, then an English professor at the University of Denver and a civil rights scholar, started the process officially in 2006 by recording dozens of interviews with me and taping my presentations to her class. Those interviews and much of Margaret's subsequent research helped to provide the foundation for this book. She also traveled with me to Southfield, Michigan, and recorded an interview with my childhood friend Herbert Monts, whom I believe was wrongly convicted in the bombing of my family's home in February 1960. My initial conversation with Herbert after contacting him in 2003, the discussion recorded by Margaret, and later interviews of Herbert were all combined into the segment of chapter 16 that is written in Herbert's voice.

The family stories shared in the book are based mostly

on my recollections and those of my family members. But some of the family history described in the first chapter is based on genealogical research conducted over several years by my sister Tina Walls.

The narrative on the history of Paul Laurence Dunbar Junior and Senior High School was drawn from many sources, primarily the old Central High School Museum, which was located in a refurbished Magnolia gas station; the National Dunbar History Project, a traveling exhibit that resulted from a collaboration between the National Dunbar Alumni Association and the Special Collection/ Archives of the Ottenheimer Library at the University of Arkansas at Little Rock; Mary S. Hoffschwelle's book *The Rosenwald Schools of the American South*, published in 2006 by University Press of Florida; and, of course, my personal experiences and those of my family members who both attended and worked at the school.

I used old newspaper clippings, particularly the *Arkansas Gazette*, to jog my memory in some cases, as well as to cross-check my recollection of the court battles and the political and social upheaval swirling around me during that time. The following two memoirs and biography also were very helpful for their perspectives: *The Long Shadow of Little Rock* by Daisy Bates; *Warriors Don't Cry* by Melba Pattillo Beals; and *Faubus: The Life and Times of an American Prodigal* by Roy Reed.

Also helpful in transporting me back to my days at Central were the photographs, papers, and other files of Daisy Bates and Elizabeth Huckaby, archived in the Special Collections Division of the University of Arkansas Libraries in Fayetteville.

# ACKNOWLEDGMENTS

**Carlotta Walls LaNier**

This book would not have been possible without my wonderful family, friends, and supporters who have encouraged me from beginning to end and reached out to help in so many ways. First, to Mother, thank you for your quiet strength and for helping to make me who I am. You and Daddy were a great team. I've never stopped missing him, but I know he is smiling down on us all from heaven. Loujuana and Tina, I realize that my Central journey uprooted you in your formative years, but you moved on without complaint, accomplished great things, and lived your lives with grace and dignity. I feel fortunate to be your older sister, and I am proud of all of your accomplishments. To Ike, Whitney, and Brooke, thank you for your love, support, and patience over the years. You gave me the time and space I needed to finally be able to tell my story, and you've allowed me to tell it this way. My love for you is everlasting. And to the rest of my family—the aunts and uncles who helped to raise me, the many cousins who have shared my life, the in-laws who are as close as blood kin, my nieces and nephews and great-nieces and great-nephews, whose very existence made it necessary for me to tell this story—I carry all of you in my heart.

I also owe deep gratitude to

—Herbert Monts and the Monts family. I hope that revealing the truth of what happened to you during those dark days in Little Rock starts a healing process.

—Karol Merten, a retired associate communications professor at the University of Denver, who for twenty years never stopped telling me that I should write a book.

—Jacquelyn Benton, a professor of Africana Studies at Metropolitan State College of Denver, whose excitement and encouragement fueled the fire early on.

—Margaret Whitt, whose persistence, contacts, and guidance finally helped me to get this done. You will retire as "chief of posse" after the North Carolina book tour.

—Leslie Trumble, director of the Visual Media Center in the School of Art and Art History at the University of Denver, who added order to my world by putting the many photos under consideration for the book onto a single disc.

—Denise Anthony, an archivist professor in the University of Denver's School of Art and Art History, who generously helped me to preserve my tangible memories by putting together a team of students to archive the many boxes of papers, photographs, and artifacts that

I've kept from Central for half a century; her graduate students Annie Nelson, Shannon Walker, Sarah Johnson, and Emily Tormey, who put in countless volunteer hours after class to do the work; and Mary Stansbury, the Library and Information Services program director, who graciously approved the purchase of materials for the project. I could never repay you for your dedication, hard work, and professionalism.

—Dudley Delffs, vice president and publisher of trade books for Zondervan, the first publisher I approached, who took the time to read an early draft and offer suggestions. Your encouragement helped me to recognize the potential of this book.

—Brian Kracke, a representative for Pearson Custom Publishing, whose openness and honesty about the publishing industry broadened my mind to the range of options and helped me to make the right decision.

—Kira Stevens, whose wise advice led me to the perfect literary agent.

—Linda Loewenthal, my representative at the David Black Literary Agency, who saw the potential in this project and guided me expertly through the process, starting with connecting me with Lisa Frazier Page.

—Lisa Frazier Page, the writer who found the right path to help me complete this journey. Your listening skills and research enabled you to question, probe, and grasp the meaning of my emotions and words and craft them into this finished book. I will be ever grateful. I look forward to a long friendship.

—To Kevin Page Sr., Enjoli, Danielle, Kevin Jr., and Kyle, thanks for lending me your wife and mother, even on family vacations. You have been great sports during this project.

—John Turchiano of the Hotel and Restaurant Employees Local 6, whose encouragement, introductions, support, and suggestions were invaluable.

—Melody Guy, my editor at Ballantine/One World, whose passion for this project and great editing suggestions helped to make the book better. Your parents carried on the torch for the Little Rock Nine when they rose those early mornings in the late 1970s, escorted you to your bus stop, and watched you set off for a twenty-five-mile journey to get the best possible education. It makes my journey seem worth it to see you—such a talented and accomplished young woman—living the legacy.

—Porscha Burke, Melody's assistant, whose sense of organization, enthusiasm, and persistence kept this project on task from start to finish. Your knowledge of the process and your cheerful attitude impressed me greatly and assured me that the book was in good hands.

—The staff at the William J. Clinton Foundation, particularly Helen Robinson, whose friendship and wise guidance helped to get many areas of this book locked down; Laura Graham, whose intervention and professionalism iced the cake; and Ana Maria Coronel, whose assistance and follow-through kept things flowing smoothly.

—Johanna Miller, a historian at the University of Arkansas, whose invaluable insight, research, and willingness to help cannot be measured.

—Michael Madell, National Park Service superintendent at the Little Rock Central High School Memorial Site, whose encouragement and focus helped me through the many projects we shared.

—Laura Miller of the National Park Service, who gave me the possibilities to publish; however, I am glad I waited.

—Spirit Trickey, whose enthusiasm never waned.

—James "Skip" Rutherford, dean of the Clinton School of Public Service, who has helped whenever and wherever I needed it. Our business relationship started with a handshake in 1996, but it has developed into a lasting friendship. From Skip to Dean Skip—what growth!

—Bunny and Peggy, my best buddies, who have been an integral part of my life forever.

—The Denver chapter of the Links Inc., my sisters, who have always been there for me.

—Melba, whose willingness to share a wealth of expertise and experiences will never be forgotten (even though I did not quite follow "the program").

—My eight comrades and friends (Elizabeth, Ernie,

Gloria, Jefferson, Melba, Minnijean, Terrence, and Thelma), for enduring the journey.

## Lisa Frazier Page

I thank God for the generations of civil rights warriors, particularly Carlotta and her eight comrades, who with great personal sacrifice and suffering kicked down the doors that I have walked through. It has been the honor of my life, Carlotta, to help you share your powerful, historic story. Thank you for trusting me and opening your life to me. I am grateful for the wonderful friendship that has developed. Thanks, too, Ike, Whitney, and Brooke, for sharing your wife and mother with me these many months.

To my literary agent, Linda Loewenthal of the David Black Literary Agency, you have been an awesome adviser and representative. I will be forever grateful to you for connecting me with Carlotta and this wonderful opportunity.

To the staff at Ballantine/One World and Random House that had a hand in producing this book, thank you for putting so much care and consideration into every step of the process. I'm especially grateful to our editor, Melody Guy, whose thoughtfulness, passion, and great ideas helped to refine the book; and Porscha Burke, who was always there with the right answers, a kind spirit, and a quiet assertiveness that kept things moving on time.

I could not have done this without the support of my husband, Kevin Page, and our children—Enjoli, Danielle, Kevin Jr., and Kyle—who fill my days with purpose. You remind me what's really important. I love you all beyond measure.

I am forever indebted to my parents, Clinton and Nettie Frazier, who gave me the diary where I first learned to tell stories. Your love and support have been a steady source of strength in my life. Thanks also to the rest of my family, who have always been there for me, especially my sister and brother-in-law (Melissa and Zeke Moses), my brother and sister-in-law (Clifford and Tiffani Frazier), Aunt Joyce (Joyce Richardson), Buffy (April Bruns), and all of my nieces and nephews. I have been blessed, too, with wonderful in-laws, particularly my husband's parents, Richard and Miriam Page, who have been patient and understanding (especially those times when I've had to "borrow" your office all day during family visits). I've appreciated every word of encouragement and home-cooked meal, and the moments you, Kolin, and Geraldine (my brother- and sister-in-law) or Zina (my sister-in-law) entertained the children while I worked.

To my life mentors, Ada Hannibal Green and the late Barbara Butler, thank you for seeing something worthwhile in me early on and investing your time and heart to open the world beyond Bogalusa to me through my girlhood travels with you and the Spartanette Service Club.

I am also grateful to work at the *Washington Post*, where my editors generously granted me the time away to do this important work, even as our industry was experiencing tremendous change and uncertainty. Thanks especially to my editors: Milton Coleman for your early encouragement and advice; Tom Wilkinson for your enthusiasm about the project and kind words; and Robert McCartney and Phyllis Jordan, for letting me go and welcoming me back. Thanks also to my journalism colleagues and cherished friends, who eagerly read chapter drafts, advised and encouraged me, and even babysat, most especially Wil Haygood, Karima and Dion Haynes, Cheryl Thompson, Donald Washington, Avis Thomas-Lester, Deneen Brown, Lonnae O'Neal Parker, Tracey Reeves, Tammy Collins Carter, and Keith Woods.

To my dear friend Lavette Broussard, who fills in for my out-of-town family, I'm grateful for all you do. And to the girls (and guy) who grew up with me into adulthood—Deadra Courtney (Ann), Veronica Smith, Cassandra Price, Kelvin Preston, and Tess Snipes—I value all we've shared and learned along the way.

# ABOUT THE AUTHORS

CARLOTTA WALLS LANIER attended Michigan State University and graduated from Colorado State College—now the University of Northern Colorado. She, along with the other members of the Little Rock Nine, received the Congressional Gold Medal, the Spingarn Medal from the NAACP, and the Lincoln Leadership Prize, awarded by the Lincoln Presidential Foundation. Marquette University conferred the Père Marquette Discovery Award, its highest honor, on the Little Rock Nine on February 9, 2010. Others to receive this award include Archbishop Desmond Tutu, Mother Teresa, Rev. Karl Rahner, and the Apollo 11 astronauts. She was inducted into the Colorado Women's Hall of Fame and the National Women's Hall of Fame and is the recipient of five honorary doctorate degrees. Carlotta lives in Colorado and is active in numerous community organizations there.

LISA FRAZIER PAGE, a professional-in-residence at Louisiana State University, is a former editor and award-winning reporter at the *Washington Post*. She is coauthor of the *New York Times* bestseller *The Pact: Three Young Men Make a Promise and Fulfill a Dream,* and she has collaborated on several other books. A graduate of Dillard University in New Orleans, Page holds a master's degree from Northwestern University's Medill School of Journalism. She lives in the New Orleans metropolitan area with her husband. They have four adult children.